DISCIPLE

FAST TRACK

Into the Word, Into the World

LUKE-ACTS
STUDY MANUAL

Dıscıple FAST TRACK
Luke-Acts Study Manual
Copyright © 2017 by Abingdon Press
Dıscıple: ınto the word, ınto the world
Study Manual, copyright © 1991 by Cokesbury
Second Edition, copyright © 2001 by Abingdon Press
All rights reserved.

Writers: Richard Byrd Wilke and Julia Kitchens Wilke
Consultant to the Writers: William Power and Leander E. Keck
General Editors: Susan Wilke Fuquay and Elaine Friedrich

17 18 19 20 21 22 23 24 25 26—10 9 8 7 6 5 4 3 2 1
Manufactured in the United States of America

DISCIPLE FAST TRACK

CONTENTS

As You Continue DISCIPLE FAST TRACK

You are beginning the second part of a four-part study. As you may know, DISCIPLE FAST TRACK: BECOMING DISCIPLES THROUGH BIBLE STUDY covered the whole Bible, Genesis through Revelation. This study, DISCIPLE FAST TRACK: INTO THE WORD, INTO THE WORLD, will slow down and go deeper into Genesis and Exodus, Luke and Acts. The third study, DISCIPLE FAST TRACK: REMEMBER WHO YOU ARE, covers the Prophets and the Letters of Paul. The fourth study, DISCIPLE FAST TRACK: THE TREE OF LIFE, covers the Writings, John, and Revelation. So after completion of all four parts of the study, the Bible has been covered twice.

In this second study, you are entering familiar territory. The format of the Study Manual is familiar to you, though some features are new. They are explained below. Familiarity means you will be at home in the commitment you are now making of about thirty minutes a day for disciplined study and seventy-five minutes of participation in the group meeting.

The study is based on the Common English Bible (CEB). We recommend everyone have a study Bible because of the additional study aids included, such as explanatory notes and maps.

The daily reading assignments are shorter than in the first study, but you will be studying Scripture in greater detail. You will also be encouraged to spend an increased amount of time practicing the spiritual disciplines highlighted in each session.

As you write your daily reflections on Scripture, include your thoughts on what Scripture is saying about your ministry in the world. You will use these notes later in the week in "God's Word in My World."

Spiritual Disciplines

In each session we practice two spiritual disciplines in addition to the study of Scripture and prayer. They are Sabbath and an additional practice that changes each session. The practice of spiritual disciplines can bring order to life and keep Bible study related to witness and service in the world. The spiritual discipline each session emerges from the session's Scripture reading.

Sabbath-keeping is a way of sorting out priorities, of trusting God. Each session's Sabbath emphasis will inform your decision about how you remember the Sabbath and ultimately about how you will live out the other six days of the week. Sabbath-keeping is not meant to be a new legalism; it is a gift of rest and freedom.

Into the World

In this section some ministry needs in the world are identified along with suggested responses. Commitment to ministry in the world is a commitment to choosing a lifestyle informed by Scripture. It involves conversion of attitudes and perspectives, and it sends persons into the world as servant-ministers.

God's Word in My World

This section invites you to summarize the Scripture message you have heard in order to shape your daily thoughts, attitudes, and actions to become more like Christ. Then, you will be challenged to commit to integrate your response into daily living by following a specific, measurable action.

DISCIPLE
FAST TRACK

LUKE-ACTS

"Now, master, let your servant go in peace according to
your word,
because my eyes have seen your salvation.
You prepared this salvation in the presence of all peoples.
It's a light for revelation to the Gentiles
and a glory for your people Israel."   —Luke 2:29-32

1 Good News for the Whole World

OUR HUMAN CONDITION

Despair darkens the sky. Is there any hope? It feels like nothing will ever get better. Perhaps some things take place "in God's time." Who knows the moment a baby is to be born? Maybe God is active but am I missing it? I get preoccupied with other matters. How can I be ready to receive from God?

My commitment for "God's Word in My World" from our last session is:

ASSIGNMENT

As you read the assigned Scriptures this week, read slowly to spot unusual side stories. Look for Jewish customs and rituals. Watch as subthemes are introduced. Be aware of parallels between John the Baptist and Jesus.

SPIRITUAL DISCIPLINES

Study

Through our disciplined reading and study of Scripture and the resulting insights, God works to change us.

How do I expect God to change me through my study?

How will I practice this spiritual discipline this week?

Sabbath

Sabbath reminds us of the continuing covenant between God and people made known in a special way in Jesus Christ. As you observe Sabbath, recall that Jesus said Sabbath was made for people, not people for Sabbath.

Prayer

Pray daily before study:

"Save your people, God!
    Bless your possession!
    Shepherd them and carry them for all time!"
                (Psalm 28:9).

Prayer concerns for the week:

Day 1 **Read Luke 1:1-25, 57-80** (birth of John).

Day 2 **Read Luke 3:1-20; 7:18-35** (John's ministry and question to Jesus); **Matthew 14:1-12; Luke 9:7-9** (John's death).

Day 3 **Read Luke 1:26-56** (Annunciation and Magnificat); **Luke 2:1-20** (birth of Jesus).

Day 4 **Read Luke 2:21-52** (Jesus in the Temple, as a baby, at twelve).

Day 5 **Read Luke 3:21-38** (baptism of Jesus, Jesus' genealogy); **Luke 4:1-13** (temptation in the wilderness).

Day 6 **Read "Into the Word" and "Into the World" and answer the questions or provide responses.**

Day 7 **Rest, pray, and attend class.**

DISCIPLE FAST TRACK

INTO THE WORD

Who is Jesus? Luke wants us to know. So he arranged his material, selected hymns and prophecy that help depict the kind of Savior Jesus is.

The Birth of John the Baptist

Why does Luke's Gospel begin with John the Baptist? Because Luke wants us to understand clearly that Jesus is firmly grounded in Israel. Basic to Jewish belief about Messiah was that Elijah, or one like Elijah, would come as a forerunner to prepare the way. Even today, in the Jewish Seder meal at Passover, the faithful pause to look for Elijah.

John's father, Zechariah, and his mother, Elizabeth, were pious folk, both descendants of Aaron. They lived in a little town in the southern hills of Judea (Luke 1:65). Zechariah was a priest. A village priest would be called to Jerusalem twice a year to help for a week in the Temple. Then they would draw lots to see who might offer the sacrifice or burn the incense. Out of the eight hundred or so priests available each week, a man might never be chosen for a significant task.

Zechariah's lot was drawn to offer prayers for all Israel by lighting the incense, morning and evening. What a privilege. What were his prayers? Besides his pastoral obligations, he had a personal heartache. Elizabeth was barren. A picture of Jewish devotion, this childless couple, in the eyes of the people, must be in disfavor with God. Under the Law, barrenness was grounds for divorce. Elizabeth stood in the tradition of Sarah, Rebekah, Rachel, Samson's mother, and Hannah, all of whom, as they grew older, pleaded with God for a child.

A messenger of God appeared. Notice the familiar pattern. The angel told Zechariah not to be afraid. Elizabeth will bear a son; there will be great joy. He must be raised a Nazirite, like Samson and Samuel. The rules about Nazirites are in Numbers 6:1-8. As usual in divine visions of this nature. Zechariah expressed doubt, for he and Elizabeth were getting old. The angel Gabriel reaffirmed the promise but made him unable to speak until the child's birth because he had doubted.

Zechariah left the Temple and returned home. Soon Elizabeth conceived. She said the Lord "has shown his favor to me by removing my disgrace among other people" (Luke 1:25). When the son was born, all the relatives and neighbors in their little village rejoiced (a common theme in Luke). They came on the eighth day for the circumcision and naming of the baby (1:59-60).

Custom ruled a Judean village. Of course the boy would be named after his father, or at least after his grandfather. But no, Elizabeth said the child's name was John, meaning "God shows favor." John comes from *Johanan*, a name used in the priestly line of Zadok. The neighbors were puzzled. "What then will this child be?" (Luke 1:66).

His tongue loosed, the old man burst into words of praise. "Bless the Lord God of Israel" (1:68). The hymn is now called "Benedictus" for the first word in the Latin translation. Old Testament imagery abounds.

Zechariah referred to John, his son, as a prophet of the Most High. "You will go before the Lord to prepare his way," he said. To do what? "You will tell his people how to be saved through the forgiveness of their sins" (Luke 1:76-77). So he grew up, not drinking any wine, not cutting his hair, avoiding everything dead—human or animal—living in the wilderness, existing off the desert until the time for his public ministry to begin (1:80).

The Ministry of John

Let us now follow John's ministry before studying Jesus' birth. In Luke 3:1-2 Luke gives us the full range of political and religious leaders in his world. John began to preach his message of repentance to everyone who would listen—Jews, Romans, Greeks, Samaritans. His baptism was not the Jewish baptism for converts to Judaism. He asked for repentance, for a change of life. Divine forgiveness was symbolized by baptism in the Jordan. His was a frightful message: "You children of snakes! Who warned you to escape from the angry judgment that is coming soon? Produce fruit that shows you have changed your hearts and lives" (3:7-8). The time of judgment was imminent; the time to repent and change was now. It was not enough simply to be a Jew, a child of Abraham.

John continually stressed that he was a voice "crying out in the wilderness: / 'Prepare the way for the Lord'" (3:4). His baptism was only water, symbol of inner repentance and spiritual cleansing. One greater than he was coming who would baptize with the Holy Spirit and fire.

The promised one, said John, would bring complete judgment, separating the wheat from the husks (chaff) (3:17).

Notice how John rooted his message in the law of Moses. If you have two coats, share one. Break bread with the needy. Be honest in business. Don't extort money from the poor. He reminded them of the Ten Commandments.

He used Herod Antipas as a gross example of adultery. In Matthew 14:1-12 Herod's stepdaughter (identified by Josephus, the Jewish historian, as Salome) danced for him and asked for John's head on a platter as a reward. Herod hesitated for two reasons: First, prophets in Israel always received a certain deference; but more, his political ambitions and standing with Rome would be harmed by killing a man so popular with the people.

He fulfilled Salome's demand, however, and had John beheaded. Later, after Jesus' crucifixion, when Herod went to Rome asking to be king, he was rebuffed by the emperor. He was exiled along with Herodias to the frontier territory of Gaul.

While John was still in prison, he sent disciples to ask Jesus straight out if he were really the one to come. Jesus' reply picked up the signs of the Kingdom that both he and John were expecting to be fulfilled (Luke 7:18-35). As for John, Jesus said to the crowds,

"What did you go out into the wilderness to see? A stalk blowing in the wind?" (7:24). On the contrary, John the Baptist stood in the tradition of fearless prophets—Nathan before King David, Elijah before King Ahab.

The Annunciation

Luke, the doctor, indicates Elizabeth was in her sixth month of pregnancy when the angel spoke to Mary (Luke 1:26). Mary was betrothed, a legally binding engagement, usually made by the parents, broken only by divorce or death. Read Deuteronomy 22:13-21 to understand how strict the law was that a girl be a virgin. Joseph was a descendant of King David, and Mary probably was also, so Bethlehem was their family city.

When the angel greeted Mary, he told her not to be afraid. "You will . . . give birth to a son, and you will name him Jesus" (Luke 1:31). The name *Jesus* is a Greek derivative of *Joshua*, meaning "God saves."

"How will this happen since I haven't had sexual relations with a man?" Mary asked (1:34). A wondrous expression now comes from the angel. "The Holy Spirit will come over you and the power of the Most High will overshadow you" (1:35). Do you remember the cloud of God's Presence that overshadowed the Tabernacle?

When we read about God's call to Moses in the Old Testament portion of this study, we heard Moses' lame excuses. Isaiah's response to God's call was "Mourn for me!" Jeremiah protested that he was only a boy. No one in the Bible, except Jesus himself, made so full a surrender, showed such willingness to serve, as did Mary in her response to God. "I am the Lord's servant. Let it be with me just as you have said" (1:38).

Mary hurried to see her relative. When Elizabeth saw her, the baby (John the Baptist) leaped in her womb as if he already recognized the Savior (1:43-44). The two women shared a common experience: They both were caught up in the mystery of God; they both were pregnant. We can imagine they laughed together in that tiny village in the hills of Judea. The one woman was old. Her son, tough like Amos, intense like Elijah, would end the old era. The other woman was young, a virgin. Her son, greater even than Moses or the prophets, would usher in the new era.

In Mary's song, called the "Magnificat" from the first word in the Latin translation, seeds of spiritual revolution sprout forth: "He has scattered those with arrogant thoughts and proud inclinations" (1:51). A political revolution brews: "He has pulled the powerful down from their thrones" (1:52). An economic revolution looms on the horizon: "He has filled the hungry" and "sent the rich away empty-handed" (1:53). A revolution would occur in Jesus that would transform human attitudes, topple empires, and cause economic systems to be turned upside down.

Where do you see evidence of this revolution in the world today?

The Birth of Jesus

Luke 2:1 begins the familiar Christmas story, but Luke was less interested in the details of nativity than he was in teaching who Jesus is. Luke located the event historically within the forty years of relative peace under the Roman emperor Augustus. He fixed the place as Bethlehem, reminding us that Jesus was descended from King David.

The baby was born in a barn or cave, wrapped in peasant cloth, and laid in a feed trough. What person, no matter how poor or oppressed, could be intimidated by so humble a child? God announced the glorious event to shepherds, the lowest of the low. The shepherds were generally hirelings, poorly paid, who found it impossible to keep ceremonially clean and who could seldom go to synagogue or Temple. They were not looked upon as good Jews. God saw to it that the poor heard the good news first. The words *Savior* and *Christ* jump out of the angel's announcement to the shepherds (2:11).

Luke, the Gentile evangelist, carefully commented that Joseph and Mary completed the Jewish rituals according to the laws of Moses (2:22). In accordance with the custom of Abraham and the law of Moses, the parents took Jesus for circumcision and naming on the eighth day (2:21).

Two further sacrifices were required. The religious law honored the first fruits of harvest and the firstborn child or animal. The male child first opening the womb would receive a double portion of his father's possessions, the father's blessing, and succession to authority. The child was offered to God and then redeemed, or bought back, to remember that God had spared the firstborn Hebrews when death passed over them in Egypt. The redemption price was five silver shekels in Hebrew money, to be paid one month after birth. Because Roman money was not allowed in the Temple, money changers in the Temple traded Roman money for Hebrew shekels so that the coins could be used in Jewish worship.

Religious law required another ritual, the sacrifice of purification (Leviticus 12:2-8). A woman who had given birth was ceremonially unclean until she offered sacrifices about forty days after the birth of a son, twice that many days after the birth of a daughter. Imagine the tremendous hardship for the poor or for those who lived at a distance to travel to the Temple with a new baby to offer sacrifices. Apparently Mary and Joseph combined the two, redeeming the firstborn and offering the purification sacrifice at the same time. The usual sacrifice, a lamb and a turtledove or pigeon, was expensive. Special provision was made for women in humble circumstances who could not afford a lamb. They could offer two turtledoves or pigeons, a compassionate rule (12:8). That was what Mary did. The mother of Jesus could give only the offering of the poor.

A devout old man named Simeon had spent his life praying for the Messiah. Many such people lived in Israel. Simeon was convinced that he would not die until he had seen the Christ. He took the child in his arms, praised God and said, "My eyes have seen your salvation" for "all peoples," declaring revelation and glory

NOTES

11

for Gentiles and Jews (Luke 2:29-32). His song in Christian liturgy is called the "Nunc Dimittis," from the Latin translation of "now dismiss."

Simeon cast the shadows of the cross on the child. Some people would rise, but some would fall; and Jesus would reveal the secret thoughts of the heart. A sword would pierce the innermost being of Mary (2:34-35). Then an eighty-four-year-old widow named Anna, who practically lived in the Temple, praying and fasting, also saw the child. She knew immediately that she had seen the one who was to redeem Jerusalem. Mary and Joseph had performed everything "required by the Law of the Lord" (2:39).

We can assume that Jesus had celebrated his *bar mitzvah* in Nazareth. He came to Jerusalem at the age of twelve as a man of Israel, a "son of the law." He sat with the teachers in the Temple. But when the time came to go home, Jesus was not with the group of pilgrims. Mary and Joseph had to go looking for him. What parents has not lost a child in a crowd? How human of Mary to say, "Your father and I have been worried" (2:48). Yet Jesus' sonship focused now on his Father God. He started as a baby in the Jerusalem Temple, his Father's house; he would return to Jerusalem as the Human One (Son of Man) to die there.

Jesus Made Ready

Jesus was baptized, as Matthew's Gospel puts it, "to fulfill all righteousness" (Matthew 3:15). Luke is less interested in the form of the event than in the meaning, for the Holy Spirit came in power "like a dove" upon Jesus, affirming his divine sonship (Luke 3:22), proclaiming him God's Christ to the world.

Jesus did not wander from the water of baptism to wilderness any more than the Israelites strayed into Sinai. He was "led by the Spirit" (4:1). What kind of a Savior was he to be? What would be his message, his style, his deeds? So little time. Every act, every word must proclaim and usher in God's kingdom.

The forty days and nights of fasting and prayer brought Jesus to physical and spiritual vulnerability. Now he did not hear God's voice declaring, "You are my Son" (3:22). Now he heard the devil speak. The first words challenged him: "Since you are God's Son . . . " (4:3).

The temptations were real, as temptations are real for us. The first temptation was economic. Jesus could minister by helping the poor, feeding the hungry. A desperate need, then and now. But Jesus knew that manna by itself does not fully satisfy. We are called to live totally dependent—breath by breath, step by step, trusting in God's word, even as the Israelites were dependent in the wilderness. Jesus quoted Moses, "People don't live on bread alone. No, they live based on whatever the LORD says" (Deuteronomy 8:3). Bread is necessary; faith is eternal.

The second temptation was political. The pious Jews were petitioning God for Messiah, a king like David, who would drive out the Roman army, restore Jewish coins with palm branches on them instead of Caesar's face. Every Jew felt the crushing oppression of the foreigners. Political uprising would require all the intrigue, the violence, the political compromise of the world. It would require the devil's own strategies. Again Jesus quoted Deuteronomy: "It's written, *You will worship the Lord your God and serve only him*" (Luke 4:8).

The third temptation was religious. The people would demand a sign, a wonder, a dramatic demonstration of supernatural power. Would it get their attention if he jumped off the top of the Temple? Would miracles really convert people? Notice that the devil fortified his argument by quoting Psalm 91:11-12. Look in Exodus 17:1-7 for the full context of Jesus' reply to the devil. Jesus, tutored by that spiritual tragedy, quoted Moses: "Don't test the Lord your God" (Luke 4:12; see Deuteronomy 6:16).

The direction of ministry had been determined. The Savior, the Messiah, had come. His mission had been defined. Jesus returned to Galilee filled with "the power of the Spirit" (Luke 4:14), ready to begin his mighty work.

INTO THE WORLD

Luke makes sure we know that Jesus was a Jew, that Mary and Joseph fulfilled the requirements of the law of Moses, that both Temple and synagogue were infused into Jesus' experience.

How familiar are you with Judaism? Are you open to learning about and appreciating Jewish traditions and customs?

How do you see God's activity in the world?

How do you prepare to receive what God has for you?

God's Word in My World

In what new ways will this session's message from God's Word influence my daily thoughts, attitudes, and actions so I continue to become more like Christ?

I will commit to integrating the above response into my daily living beginning this week by following this specific, measurable action:

IF YOU WANT TO KNOW MORE

Compare the baptism and temptation stories in the Synoptic Gospels: Matthew 3:13-17; 4:1-11; Mark 1:9-13; Luke 3:21-22; 4:1-13. Read the Prologue to John's Gospel (John 1:1-18) for a greatly different introduction to Jesus' ministry. Notice John's reference to John the Baptist as one who came to bear witness (John 1:6-7).

"And I tell you: Ask and you will receive. Seek and you will find. Knock and the door will be opened to you."

—Luke 11:9

2 Teach Us to Pray

OUR HUMAN CONDITION

We feel totally alone and lonely. Something in our hearts tells us we are not complete until we communicate with the eternal, the infinite. We cry out for help. We need to know our cry will be heard.

My commitment for "God's Word in My World" from our last session is:

ASSIGNMENT

The assignments this week will be different. You will read a section of the Study Manual daily. As you go through each of the topics, you will be directed to read various Scripture verses. Be sure to respond to the questions each day as well.

SPIRITUAL DISCIPLINES

Prayer

As we pray for ourselves and for others, our spiritual life is strengthened and power is set loose in the lives of those for whom we pray.

What will give order and discipline to my praying?

How will I practice this discipline this week?

Sabbath

On the specified day, go apart for a time of prayer. Make a list of concerns and of persons for whom you want to pray. Pray for people you normally overlook and for the needs of the larger community and world. Try writing a prayer of intercession for ongoing use.

Prayer

Pray daily before study:

"Let my cry reach you, Lord;
   help me understand according to what
      you've said.
Let my request for grace come before you;
   deliver me according to your promise!"
                    (Psalm 119:169-170).

Prayer concerns for the week:

Day 1 Read in your Study Manual the section titled "Day 1: Jesus' Prayer Life." Read the Bible verses indicated and answer the questions.

Day 2 Read in your Study Manual the section titled "Day 2: Prayers of Intercession and Agony." Read the Bible verses indicated and answer the questions.

Day 3 Read in your Study Manual the section titled "Day 3: The Lord's Prayer." Read the Bible verses indicated and answer the questions.

Day 4 Read in your Study Manual the section titled "Day 4: The Lord's Prayer Continued." Read the Bible verses indicated and answer the questions.

Day 5 Read in your Study Manual the section titled "Day 5: Other Teachings About Prayer." Read the Bible verses indicated and answer the questions.

Day 6 Read in your Study Manual the sections titled "Day 6: Into the World" and "God's Word in My World." Answer the questions or provide responses.

Day 7 Rest, pray, and attend class.

INTO THE WORD

In Luke every moment of Jesus' ministry is marked by prayer. No other Gospel writer so consistently shines his spotlight on the prayers of Jesus.

Day 1: Jesus' Prayer Life

"When everyone was being baptized, Jesus also was baptized. While he was praying, heaven was opened and the Holy Spirit came down on him in bodily form like a dove" (read Luke 3:21-22; compare Matthew 3:16; Mark 1:9-11).

Jesus was baptized in the Jordan River, probably between Jericho and the Dead Sea. He then walked into the wilderness of the Judean desert, where he fasted and struggled with the precise direction his ministry would take (read Luke 4:1-13). If baptism empowered him, wilderness directed him. Do not underestimate this crucial period when Jesus placed his ministry before God.

When have you experienced a time when you felt empowered from the Holy Spirit to serve?

What temptations did you have that hindered your service?

Another great moment of prayer came when Jesus took Peter, James, and John up on the mountain, either Mount Tabor or Mount Hermon, to pray (read Luke 9:28-36). "As he was praying, the appearance of his face changed and his clothes flashed white like lightning" (9:29; recall Moses on Sinai in Exodus 34:29-30). Jesus Christ incorporated the law (Moses) and the prophets (Elijah). The experience indicated that both Moses and Elijah affirmed his ministry, which was taking him to Jerusalem and death on the cross.

How does spending time in the presence of God change you?

Table fellowship meant deep friendship and community in Israel. Bread symbolized manna, the providence of God. For Jesus, breaking bread was always a holy moment, never to be experienced without prayer. Surrounded by five thousand hungry listeners, he took five loaves and two fish, "looked up to heaven, blessed them, and broke them" (read Luke 9:12-17).

Jesus thanked God for the five loaves and two fish. It was not until after the meal that the miracle was realized. How are you able to thank God for what you have now?

NOTES

In the Passover meal, it was the custom for the host to break the bread with prayer. And it was Jesus' custom to give thanks for the bread *before* he broke the loaf (22:19). Was it Jesus' way of blessing bread and breaking it that caused the two followers in Emmaus to recognize him (read Luke 24:28-35)? Jesus was made known to them in the breaking of the bread. How has Jesus been made known to you when praying and breaking bread with others?

Luke slowly helps us see that Jesus was a person of prayer. He went to the synagogue, a place of prayer and study, "as he normally did" (4:16). Sometimes he seemed to pray alone while the disciples were with him (9:18). Sometimes he went aside and prayed all night (6:12). Share a powerful experience of when you have prayed alone.

Share a powerful experience of when you have prayed with others.

Striking is Luke's phrase right before the dramatic prayer in Gethsemane when Jesus prayed so hard and so long: "Jesus left and made his way to the Mount of Olives, as was his custom" (22:39).

Notice "when he arrived" (22:40). Where? The normal place for prayers? Look at 21:37. He urged the disciples to pray that they might not fail the coming test. "He withdrew from them about a stone's throw, knelt down, and prayed" (22:41).

Who among us does not pray before making important decisions? One of the Lord's most significant decisions was choosing his twelve disciples. On them would rest his message and his mission. They would bear the witness on which his church would be built. Apparently he had a group of followers whom he had been teaching. Now was the time to pick the leadership, the Twelve, representing the tribes of Israel. He went to a mountainside to pray, and he prayed all night long. On the following day he named the ones he had chosen (read Luke 6:12-16).

Our Lord encouraged us to ask, to search, to knock (11:9-10). He himself asked God for counsel and for power to heal. In Mark's Gospel the disciples asked why *they* could not heal the boy with epilepsy. Jesus, who had just returned from the mountain of prayer, said, "Throwing this kind of spirit out requires prayer" (Mark 9:29). We pray for the sick and with the sick, but Jesus seems to have prayed ahead of time, pleading for power that came available to him when the need arose.

When Jesus received the seventy* (remember Jacob took seventy into Egypt), observe what happened to his prayers. They were transformed into adulation and praise. We often petition, then

* Other ancient authorities say "seventy-two."

Disciple FAST TRACK

neglect to praise. The seventy returned with joy, having healed, converted, and cast out demons (Luke 10:17). "At that very moment, Jesus overflowed with joy from the Holy Spirit and said, 'I praise you, Father'" (10:21). How do you ask, seek, or knock in a spirit of prayer?

Day 2: Prayers of Intercession and Agony

Prayer for others seems mysterious. Yet we all do pray for others. The Bible teaches that profound prayer for others has great power. Read James 5:13-16. How have you prayed for others?

From the moment our Lord set his face toward Jerusalem, Peter began to have doubts (Mark 8:32-33). The successes of the Human One attracted him; the sufferings of the Human One alienated him. He sulked at the Passover meal and was the last to have his feet washed (read John 13:3-11). He fell asleep during Jesus' prayer of agony in Gethsemane (read Luke 22:45-46). Three times he swore that he never knew Jesus (read Luke 22:56-60).

Read Luke 22:31-34. Peter claimed he was ready to go to prison, even to death. But Jesus, aware that Peter was wavering, looked him squarely in the eye and said, "Simon, Simon, look! Satan has asserted the right to sift you all like wheat. However, I have prayed for you that your faith won't fail." Imagine the power of Jesus' prayer for Peter! Jesus would also have prayed for Judas. He knew Satan was sifting all of them.

We know that God needs hands to feed a hungry child, needs witnesses to proclaim the gospel. How does intercessory prayer open doors for the Holy Spirit that would otherwise not be opened?

Can God do things if we pray that God cannot do if we do not pray? Share your ideas.

Do you remember how Aaron wore the twelve precious stones, representing the people before God as he offered prayers and sacrifices? Read Hebrews 10:11-25. It says that Jesus Christ not only has offered the perfect sacrifice for our sins but offers the priestly prayer for us continually.

In what areas of your life do you receive strength from knowing that Jesus is praying for you as he did for Peter?

The greatest prayer of petition ever offered came from Jesus' lips on the cross. He became the holy supplicant, beseeching God for us all: "Father, forgive them, for they don't know what they're doing" (Luke 23:34). No prayer in all the world has locked God and humankind together in so desperate a soul struggle as did Jesus' prayer in Gethsemane (read Luke 22:39-46). Jesus prayed so earnestly that "his sweat became like drops of blood falling on the ground" (22:44). An angel even gave him strength to pray harder (22:43). What was at stake? What was his struggle?

When have you ever needed an angel's strength to pray harder?

We scarcely think Jesus would slip out of the garden into the night, go back to Nazareth, and pick up carpentry. No, there were people with leprosy to heal, beggars who were blind to be given their sight, people who were hungry yet to be fed. Were the disciples ready? Judas had sold out. Peter, James, and John were asleep. Was this the time and place to stand firm? Also, the next few hours—trials, scourgings, betrayals, jeers, pain, death—stood starkly before him if he remained in the garden. What person would not sidestep torturous death if it were possible? Jesus prayed, "Father, if it's your will, take this cup of suffering away from me" (22:42). No one wants to die; but more, no one wants to be cut off in midlife. Is this the divine will?

Sometimes our prayers are not answered. God, "I Am Who I Am," is no idol to be cajoled, no false god to be manipulated. Jesus taught us to ask. He asked; he pleaded.

Yet in the garden he showed us the yielded prayer of submission: "Not my will but your will must be done" (22:42). When was one of the most difficult times that you have prayed this prayer?

All along he prayed, urged others to pray that he and they would not fail when the test came. He was ready, through prayer, for the trial. He stood up as the obedient Son. Luke wanted us to understand clearly that Jesus was faithful unto death. His final words were a loud cry: "Father, into your hands I entrust my life" (23:46). And he died.

How will your prayer life help sustain and keep you faithful until death?

Day 3: The Lord's Prayer

Read Luke 11:1-4. Under such spiritual tutoring, no wonder the disciples asked, "Lord, teach us to pray." Jesus' response guides all Christian prayer.

Father. The word is *Abba*—so warm, so personal that we might say "Papa" or "Dad." Judaism taught that God was near as well as high and lifted up. But "Abba" went to a deeper level of intimacy. Of all the prayers addressed to God by the religions of the world—Almighty, Holy One, God Is One—no other word expresses such depth of personal relationship like that between child and parent. What words would you use to describe your relationship with God?

Think about your relationship with God. Plot out your spiritual highs and lows in the space provided below.

What was happening in your life during the times when you felt closest to God? What was happening in your life during the time when you felt far away from God?

Uphold the holiness of your name (Hallowed be your name [NRSV]*).* "Father," though close and caring, is also righteous and just. God is mighty in power. The name and the person are one. To hold the name holy (hallowed) is to respect and revere the Holy One. In the heart of the believer, that is where God wants a perpetual sense of awe and respect. God is holy. What does holiness mean to you?

How is God holy?

Read 1 Peter 1:13-21. How are we to be holy?

Bring in your kingdom (*Your kingdom come* [NRSV]*)*. The kingdom of God is the reign or rule of God. The innocence God intended in Creation will be restored. *Shalom,* the peace and justice of God, will prevail.

Jews ask, "How could Jesus be the Messiah, for *shalom* has not yet come?" Christians respond that Jesus brought us a taste of the Kingdom. When he touched lepers, opened blind eyes, forgave penitent sinners, fed hungry people, raised the dead, he showed Kingdom signs. So we pray. We daily do the things that bring Kingdom joys. And we watch, ready and expectant. What does it mean when we say "Your kingdom come"?

What spiritual significance does that have for you?

Read Matthew 6:25-34. What do these verses tell us about what is important to Christ followers?

Day 4: The Lord's Prayer Continued
Give us the bread we need for today (*Give us each day our daily bread* [NRSV]*)*. We have learned much about manna. Jesus wants us to ask for daily bread without anxiety, to trust God for providential care. But something more is here. The prayer is communal. Broken bread is always communal. We are not taught to pray, "Give me my daily bread." We pray for bread for the people of the world. We know that manna is enough, but some jars are too full while others are empty. Methods of distribution break down. Food there is, and enough for all. The prayer intends to sensitize us to share bread with the hungry.

Read Matthew 6:31-32, Matthew 7:11, and Philippians 4:19. What do these verses tell us about God's provision?

How has God met your needs in the past?

How do you trust God for your needs today?

How do you trust God for your future needs?

Forgive us our sins, for we also forgive everyone who has wronged us (Forgive us our sins, for we ourselves forgive everyone indebted to us [NRSV]*).* Jesus interpreted this phrase himself, over and over. He knew how easy it is for us to claim mercy, how hard it is for us to extend it. Heaven and earth are yoked. As we forgive, so we are forgiven.

Read about "the unforgiving servant" (Matthew 18:23-35). What do these verses tell us about forgiveness?

Read about the keys of the Kingdom (Matthew 16:19). Notice that we control one end of the transaction even as God controls the other. What does this verse say to you about forgiving and being forgiven?

Read Jesus' explanation of this phrase in Matthew 6:14-15. Read also Mark 11:25.

Now, in Luke's Sermon on the Plain, read how we receive even as we give (Luke 6:37-38).

What do these verses teach us about forgiveness?

And don't lead us into temptation (And do not bring us to the time of trial [NRSV]). The chief point of this petition is not when and where we hit a trial, or even who put us there. The point is to ask for divine strength to stand in the midst of trial. We ask that God will not allow us to come to such a test that we will succumb. Or that God will save us in the hour of our testing. Matthew's record helps: "Rescue us from the evil one" (Matthew 6:13).

Think now about your next few days. Can you foresee trial? Where are your weak spots, your spiritual Achilles' heel? So often tests come unexpectedly. How can you be ready?

If you have not yet compared Matthew's fuller version of the Lord's Prayer, see Matthew 6:9-13. Notice that the Bible does not include "For thine is the Kingdom . . . ," which quickly became a prayer of the early church. What are the differences and similarities between the Matthew 6:9-13 version of the Lord's Prayer and the Luke 11:2-4 version?

Day 5: Other Teachings About Prayer

Prayer, like any good thing, can be misused. We can don a prayer with pride as Joseph did his long robe. Jesus warned about people who put on airs (read Luke 20:45-47). What lessons can we learn about prayer from these verses?

Of course, if they also "cheat widows out of their homes" (20:47), being hypocrites as well as egotists, their condemnation is all the greater. One unforgettable parable concerns two men who went to the Temple to pray. Read Luke 18:9-14. As you read it, remember that the Pharisee tried to live according to the full law of Moses. The Law required a fast only on the Day of Atonement once a year, yet Pharisees fasted twice a week. This man tithed on everything he acquired, not only on what he earned. Periods of prayer were scheduled during morning and evening sacrifices. Pharisees tried diligently to fulfill the Law by doing extra. Apparently the Pharisee came into the holy prayer chamber of the Temple and stood alone so he would not be contaminated by contact with other people. Jesus said that the Pharisee prayed "with himself" (18:11, RSV) or "stood by himself and prayed" (18:11, NIV).

In what ways have you prayed like a Pharisee?

What changes do you need to make in your prayer life in order to follow how God wants us to pray?

The tax collectors, or publicans, because of their dealings with the Roman government, were hated by fellow Jews. They were considered ceremonially unclean. The priests would not accept their tithes or offerings. Tax collectors were not permitted to enter the holy place of prayer, reserved for Jewish men in good standing, but stood in the courtyard reserved for women and Gentiles. Notice that Levi (5:27) and Zacchaeus (19:2) were both tax collectors.

Jesus warned his disciples repeatedly not to let down their guard. Satan waited for the right moment. An intriguing verse from Jesus' own temptation experience tells us, "After finishing every temptation, the devil departed from him until the next opportunity" (4:13). The devil waited for a high stress time such as prayer in the garden, or Judas's betrayal, or Peter's denial.

Read Matthew 25:1-13. Jesus told the parable of the ten bridesmaids, five of whom were not ready when the bridegroom came. In Luke 21:34-36 he urged his disciples always to watch and pray. Why? Our hearts can easily be weighed down with anxiety. Further, we are to be ready at all times for the day when we will stand before the Son of Man.

No command of Jesus is more difficult than his command to love our enemies. Jesus knew it would be practically impossible for us to turn the other cheek. That's why he urged us to gain God's assistance, for God is merciful, slow to anger. Read Luke 6:27-31. Notice especially "pray for those who mistreat you." What does that mean?

Not every prayer is answered with "yes," not every wish fulfilled. Sometimes the timing is not right. Often we must wait. Jesus urged us to persist in prayer. God is more willing to answer than we think. Read Luke 11:5-13. This vivid story drives the point home. In a peasant farm home, all the family might be asleep in one room, the animals and chickens asleep in the adjoining room. Imagine getting everyone quieted down. If a friend comes "at midnight," the farmer might say, "Go away" or "Do not bother me." But if the knocking persists, he will get up and give his friend bread. What does persistent prayer look like?

Read Luke 18:1-8 for an equally powerful parable. Here a judge who did not even like people granted the persistent widow a hearing so that she would not wear him out with her continual pleas. A time for surrender comes. Jesus in Gethsemane finally yielded, but not before he had prayed long and hard. What does this teach us about being persistent in prayer?

INTO THE WORLD

Day 6: Into the World

Although many prayers are spontaneous, spiritual growth results from a discipline of regular daily prayer. What time each day would be best for you? Where could you pray and be alone?

Bread should be blessed. Have grace at your meals. Eating out is a problem. So are school lunches. Talk it over. How can persons eating in public avoid either calling attention to their praying or omitting the blessing meal after meal?

Some Christians keep a prayer list so that they may pray diligently for causes of great concern or for people who are in need or are being sifted like wheat (Luke 22:31). Begin a simple list. Let it become your prayer diary. Write down thoughts of praise and thanks, special petitions, concerns. One purpose is to focus your thoughts; but another purpose is to be able to look back and rejoice in answered prayers. Do not say much about your personal prayer life, but be ready to talk about it if anyone asks, ready to teach or help if anyone requests. Maybe someone will say, "Please teach us to pray."

How might you strengthen the corporate prayer life of your DISCIPLE FAST TRACK group? your Sunday school class? your congregation?

Pray for others. In your group, pray for conversions; pray that your church will reach out to the lonely, the bewildered, the broken, the grief-stricken, the poor; pray by name for people who are spiritually wounded. Pray for the needs of the world.

When do you usually pray and where?

What is your greatest obstacle to developing your prayer life?

How can you overcome this obstacle?

God's Word in My World

In what new ways will this session's message from God's Word influence my daily thoughts, attitudes, and actions so I continue to become more like Christ?

I will commit to integrating the above response into my daily living beginning this week by following this specific, measurable action:

IF YOU WANT TO KNOW MORE

Some people sing as they pray. Some hymns are based on classic prayers or psalms. Leaf through a hymnal and sing or read some of the great prayer hymns.

"Don't judge, and you won't be judged. Don't condemn, and you won't be condemned. Forgive, and you will be forgiven. Give, and it will be given to you. A good portion—packed down, firmly shaken, and overflowing—will fall into your lap. The portion you give will determine the portion you receive in return."
—Luke 6:37-38

3 Teach Us How to Live

OUR HUMAN CONDITION

So many voices are telling us how to live. Every advertisement offers the abundant life. Some teachers seem restrictive, so filled with do's and don'ts. Some people say, "Anything goes." And then, what about criticism and rejection? I fear that if I really follow the way of Christ, friends will turn on me. How can I know the way to live?

My commitment for "God's Word in My World" from our last session is:

ASSIGNMENT

Scholars suggest that both Luke and Matthew had available to them a "Source" document of Jesus' teachings. Compare Luke 6:17-49 and Matthew 5–7. Look for similarities and variations. Each evangelist's slightly different view of Jesus results in richness of interpretation.

SPIRITUAL DISCIPLINES

Confessing

In confessing our sins and our failure to obey, we face who we are and we are set free to accept the grace and forgiveness of God.

How will I be different when I accept God's grace and forgiveness?

How will I practice this discipline this week?

Sabbath

Sabbath gives holiness to our small acts of justice and compassion. Go through your closets. Do you have used clothes in good condition that you could give to someone in need or to a clothing distribution center? Check your pantry shelves. Do you have extra food that you could share? Open your linen closet. Can you give away some towels or bedding? If you have children, have them help you. Use the moment to teach.

Prayer

Pray daily before study:

"Examine me, God! Look at my heart!
   Put me to the test! Know my anxious
      thoughts!
   Look to see if there is any idolatrous way
      in me,
      then lead me on the eternal path!"
                    (Psalm 139:23-24).

Prayer concerns for the week:

Day 1 **Read Luke 4:16–6:49** (Jesus in his home synagogue, his ministry, choosing the twelve, Sermon on the Plain).

Day 2 **Read Matthew 5–7** (Sermon on the Mount).

Day 3 **Read Luke 7–8** (healings, Jesus and John, a forgiven woman, Kingdom parables, healings).

Day 4 **Read Luke 9:1-50** (training the Twelve, Peter's confession, Transfiguration).

Day 5 **Read Luke 14:1-24** (a dinner party, a tough story about a great dinner).

Day 6 **Read "Into the Word" and "Into the World" and answer the questions or provide responses.**

Day 7 **Rest, pray, and attend class.**

DISCIPLE FAST TRACK

INTO THE WORD

NOTES

Nowhere in the Bible are we hit by words so hard as these words of Jesus. No rationalization can lessen their force. No sophisticated scholarship can free their burr-like cling. Before we try to interpret these commands, let's look at them squarely.

The Poor

"Happy are you who are poor" (Luke 6:20). Right away we are off balance. We spend our lives working, praying, trying to get out of poverty. Matthew's Gospel says "hopeless" (Matthew 5:3), but before you run to that spiritual interpretation, stay for a moment with Luke. Jesus was not blessing poverty; he was blessing the poor. "The people of the land" was what they were called. Peasants who tilled a tiny plot of rocky soil they had inherited knew what it was to sweat for a crop and lose part of it to insects, part to drought, and part to taxes.

Roman rule was economically oppressive. The tax on the land consisted of one-tenth of all grain and one-fifth of wine and oil. A tax was payable for using the roads, for owning a cart, on each wheel, on the animal that pulled it. A tax collector could force a man to stop on the road and unpack his bundles, and then would charge him whatever he wished. If the man could not pay, the collector would offer him a loan at high interest. No wonder that in popular speech murderers, robbers, and tax collectors were all grouped together.

The religious authorities also made it tough on poor people. How in the world could the poor of the land keep ceremonially clean? How could a poor mother travel to Jerusalem after every baby to offer a purification sacrifice? No wonder Jesus spoke harshly to the wealthy scribes and teachers of the law, "How terrible for you legal experts too! You load people down with impossible burdens and you refuse to lift a single finger to help them" (Luke 11:46).

People of means say, "But what about the poor who rob, the poor who are lazy, the poor who turn bitter?" Jesus was not confirming those attitudes or actions. Jesus looked with compassion on the crowd of humble, hard-working poor people of the land and said, in effect, "God wants you to have joy and blessedness, and you shall have it."

Jesus Christ was uncomfortable with an economic system in which the rich got richer and the poor got poorer. In Luke's Gospel, Jesus couples his "happys" with "terribles," point by point.

"But how terrible for you who are rich, because you have already received your comfort" (6:24).

Jesus' teachings were so hard that the disciples, who for the most part were working people, expressed astonishment. When a rich ruler came to Jesus asking to be a disciple, Jesus said, "Sell everything you own and distribute the money to the poor. . . . Come, follow me" (18:22). The man went away sad. Jesus commented, "It's very hard for the wealthy to enter God's kingdom!" (18:24).

Now the disciples were really perplexed. "Then who can be saved?" (18:26). A glimmer of hope, even for the rich, shines from Jesus' reply, "What is impossible for humans is possible for God" (18:27).

Can the rich really care about the poor? Yes, on occasion God can make it happen. Notice that Luke follows up the story of the rich ruler with the account of Zacchaeus, the rich tax collector (19:1-10).

After visiting with Jesus, Zacchaeus said, "Look, Lord, I give half of my possessions to the poor. And if I have cheated anyone, I repay them four times as much" (19:8). The impossible happened. Jesus said, "Today, salvation has come to this household" (19:9).

Now consider Matthew's "Happy are people who are hopeless." "Happy" means a peaceful, inner contentment. But why "hopeless"?

Who are the hopeless? They are the open, the receptive, the humble. Some people have "closed minds." Add smugness or self-righteousness, and you have people the gospel cannot penetrate. The other "beatitudes" are possible only if we are first receptive and humble.

But "hopeless" may also mean those whose spirits are impoverished—dispirited, depressed. In what sense can this condition be declared blessed, happy?

Jesus' Way of Life

As you compare Matthew's Sermon on the Mount with Luke's Sermon on the Plain, notice the common sayings. Scholars attribute much of this material to a collection of Jesus' teachings that both Matthew and Luke used as a source.

Teachers and theologians have struggled with these hard sayings: Impossible ethics for the world to follow, say some. An ethic for "last days," for people who thought Jesus would return soon, say others. An abolition of Moses' old laws with a totally new ethic, say still others.

But to whom was Jesus talking? Not to the world. He spoke to those who had already chosen to follow him and to those who were considering that leap of faith. In these sermons, are we not looking at a lifestyle for disciples? Jesus was not teaching people in general but giving a way of life that he expected his covenant people to follow. Why do we have difficulty basing our lifestyle on these teachings?

As for "last days"—yes and no, according to Luke's understanding. We always live expectantly, always awaiting the coming Kingdom. But in the meantime, *no matter how long,* these teachings are the guidelines for Kingdom living. Jesus himself said he did not know the hour.

Jesus emphasized the full meaning of the law of Moses. He insisted, "It's easier for heaven and earth to pass away than for the smallest stroke of a pen in the Law to drop out" (Luke 16:17). Take integrity for example. The Law said you should not bear false witness (Exodus 20:16) or break an oath (Numbers 30:2). Jesus taught his disciples to be witnesses for truth *all* the time, to be, as it were, on the witness stand every day. "Let your *yes* mean yes, and your *no* mean no" (Matthew 5:33-37; see James 5:12).

Consider divorce. Remember all the laws of Moses to protect marriage from incest, adultery, and other personal and sexual violations. "Any man who divorces his wife and marries another commits adultery, and a man who marries a woman divorced from her husband commits adultery" (Luke 16:18). In fact, Jesus argued that the marriage covenant was even deeper than the law of Moses, grounded in Creation itself (Matthew 19:3-6; Genesis 2:24).

Does this mean divorce doesn't happen? No. Moses, because of human failure, provided a law of divorce, even as we do (Matthew 5:31-32; 19:8-9). Does it mean adultery is unforgivable? No. Like lying and stealing, it can be pardoned. But it does mean that Christian disciples will do all in their power to maintain the integrity and purity of their marriages. Jesus pushed the issue to the secret recesses of the soul: "every man who looks at a woman lustfully has already committed adultery in his heart" (5:28). Evil comes out of the heart. Disciples try to keep the heart pure. But this teaching helps us be aware how fragile we all are and thus be slow to cast the first stone. The account of Jesus' treatment of the woman taken in adultery keeps the issue in compassionate balance (John 8:2-11). Radical imperative on one hand, no softening of the holiness of God; radical compassion on the other hand, no limiting of the mercy of God. Remember the ark of the covenant, with the Law inside and the cover, sometimes called the mercy seat, on top?

Jesus' Way of Life Continued

Consider anxiety or worry. We listened as the Hebrews complained in the wilderness, always worrying about whether they would have food or drink. God provided.

Jesus instructed his followers to trust God (Luke 12:22-34). Work, of course. Care for family, certainly. Plan ahead, sure. But tossing and turning in your bed, worrying about the stock market, a better job, a new car—that's the lifestyle of the heathen. All the nations are in a frenzy for more. Jesus urged us to remember the lilies and the birds and the care God gives creation: "Desire his kingdom and these things will be given to you as well" (12:31).

Consider retribution. A negative expression of the Golden Rule, "Do not do to others what you would not have them do to you" is found in rabbinic Judaism. Jesus turned it to a positive rule (6:31). The prophet Hosea remarried his wife, purchasing her from slavery after she became a harlot (Hosea 3:1-3). Forgiveness was not new to Israel.

Yet Jesus pushed forgiveness beyond any previous allowances. The Christian lifestyle avoids retribution. If a person speaks ill of you, shake it off. If someone slaps your face, turn your face for a second slap. Pray for your enemies. But observe the reason for such actions: "You will have a great reward. You will be acting the way children of the Most High act, for he is kind to ungrateful and wicked people" (Luke 6:35-36). Christ Jesus is developing a gracious people, a generous, giving people like the God they serve.

Consider judging. This teaching does not mean employers should not decide which employee to promote, that judges should not hear court cases, that artists should not discriminate among works of art, or that parents should not reprimand their children. Jesus pointed to a poison that sickens us all. To judge means to criticize, find fault, backbite, quibble, blame, tongue-lash.

Two of the Bible's most beautiful verses guide us: "Forgive, and you will be forgiven. Give, and it will be given to you" (Luke 6:37-38). The imagery now is a sack of flour, a bushel of wheat. "A good portion—packed down, firmly shaken, and overflowing—will fall into your lap. The portion you give will determine the portion you receive in return" (6:38).

The Nature of a Disciple

In both Luke's and Matthew's Gospels, the sermon concludes with the parable of the house built on a rock, or the story of the two foundations (Matthew 7:21-27; Luke 6:46-49). While it is true that this compassionate lifestyle is the way for the expectant, future-oriented community of faith, this lifestyle is also built on God and therefore on a rock. Storms will come to both houses; but the house built on criticism, anxiety, lying, will fail. The house (life) that hears the words of Jesus *and does them* will be built on a rock and will stand when the flood comes.

How can we develop such a lifestyle? It is impossible unless we love the things of God.

Four Wonderful Healings

As we consider Christian living, we must pause to comment on four special healings.

First consider the centurion's slave (Luke 7:1-10). A Roman centurion was a staff officer, career army, with one hundred soldiers under his command. This centurion had a home in Capernaum, a Jewish town on the Sea of Galilee. A worthy man, "he loves our people" and "built our synagogue for us," said the Jewish elders. His compassion showed because he tried so hard to save a slave. Still he was a Gentile, illustrating precisely the point Jesus had made in his sermon at the Nazareth synagogue (4:24-27).

The centurion's words show the strength of his belief: "Lord, . . . I don't deserve to have you come under my roof. . . . Just say the word and my servant will be healed" (7:6-7). Since it was forbidden for a Jew to go into the home of a Gentile, the soldier was being circumspect, respecting Jesus' awkward position. His sense of authority, giving Jesus credit for his spiritual power, amazed the Lord: "Even in Israel I haven't found faith like this" (7:9).

No healing story is more powerful than that of the healing of the Gerasene man possessed by demons (8:26-39). The man was mentally ill, able at times to rip off ropes, even chains, that people had used to restrain him. When Jesus found him, he was naked, frightened, living in a cemetery. Being naked and touching tombs were forbidden to Jews, but the man was so sick those things didn't matter anymore.

The demons recognized Jesus for who he really was, "Jesus, Son of the Most High God" (8:28). "What is your name?" Jesus asked, going to the heart of the matter. The man's personality was fractured. He heard many voices. He had many demons. My name is "Legion" (8:30). Six thousand soldiers made up a Roman legion. After his healing, the sick man put on clothing and sat at Jesus' feet "completely sane" (8:35).

Two other healings are interwoven (8:40-56). One is the daughter of Jairus, a leader of the synagogue. Jesus did not limit his ministry to the poor. But on the way to Jairus's home, a woman who had suffered hemorrhages for twelve years reached out and touched the fringe of Jesus' robe. She was ceremonially unclean, of course; she could not ever offer sacrifices for purification. And she was impoverished, having spent all she had on physicians. But most important, no woman would talk to or touch a man, a stranger, in public. The healing of her body occurred immediately, but notice the healing of the soul. She was hiding, trembling; she fell down before Jesus. What word did Jesus speak to the woman who had touched him in public? "Daughter" (8:48), the intimacy a father would use if his own child had touched him. He sent her on her way in peace.

Jesus had been on his way to the home of the leader of the synagogue when he stopped to heal the sick woman. Now he continued on and raised up Jairus's daughter.

Women Followers

Examine Luke 8:1-3 word for word. A social revolution was beginning that would explode in Acts. Women were accompanying the men. Some women who had been healed physically or emotionally traveled with Jesus and the Twelve to support, encourage, listen, and provide money for expenses. Mary Magdalene, who had been emotionally ill, "from whom seven demons had been thrown out," and who tradition (though not the Bible) says was a woman of the streets, was there. Joanna was of high social status, wife of Chuza, a property manager for Herod. She hurried to the tomb on Easter Sunday with Mary Magdalene

NOTES

and Mary the mother of James (24:10). Susanna is mentioned but not identified, and there were "many others" (8:3). Participation by females in Jesus' ministry is worth noting in a strongly male-dominated society. Also, the mix of social levels was a sign of Christian community. A new type of religious community was being formed.

The Turning Point

Luke 9 provides the dramatic turning point. Jesus sent the Twelve on a training mission where they brought good news and cured diseases "everywhere" (9:1-6). Herod was perplexed. He had got rid of John. What would he do with Jesus? He actually tried to see him (9:7-9).

Jesus fed the five thousand (9:12-17) as a dramatic response to human need and as a reminder that God cares and provides. Christians always pray and break bread.

But now, beginning with 9:18, there is an increased air of expectancy. Jesus was ready to tell the disciples what *Messiah* means.

When Peter declared that Jesus was "the Christ [Messiah] sent from God" (9:20), Jesus warned the disciples not to say so publicly. Then he used his own term for himself: "The Human One [Son of Man] must suffer many things" (9:22). Disciples also must be prepared to "take up their cross daily," the cross of obedient self-forgetfulness. "All who want to save their lives will lose them. But all lose their lives because of me will save them" (9:23-24).

In Luke, observe the Transfiguration (9:28-36), a reassurance from God like the Holy Spirit experience at baptism. Then followed immediately the healing of the boy with epilepsy and a statement that the disciples still did not understand: "The Human One is about to be delivered into human hands" (9:44). Quickly now, Jesus taught that the truly great are like children, and he told the disciples not to condemn those strangers who were healing in his name. Now he was ready: "As the time approached when Jesus was to be taken up into heaven, he determined to go to Jerusalem" (9:51).

INTO THE WORLD

Christians are called to live out a life worthy of the gospel of Jesus Christ. As we practice our faith in everyday situations, in small gestures, we become the hands and feet of Christ to a desperate and hurting world. How do you reach out to a hurting world?

We spend time in God's Word in order to learn how we are to live out our faith. How is God's Word teaching you how to live?

We pray so that we might develop a living relationship with God. How is your prayer life helping you learn how to live?

We think and act like Jesus so that we serve others in need. How do you live out your faith that reaches out to the world?

God's Word in My World

In what new ways will this session's message from God's Word influence my daily thoughts, attitudes, and actions so I continue to become more like Christ?

I will commit to integrating the above response into my daily living beginning this week by following this specific, measurable action.

IF YOU WANT TO KNOW MORE

Use a study Bible or look online for a guide to parallel Gospel passages to compare the teachings in Matthew 5–7 with similar passages in Mark and Luke. Look for similarities, even exact wording. Look for varieties of emphasis and interpretation.

NOTES

But he said to them, "I must preach the good news of God's kingdom in other cities too, for this is why I was sent."
—Luke 4:43

4 Signs of God's Rule

OUR HUMAN CONDITION

My rule is, Look after Number One. I ask, Will it be good for me? I expect others to do the same. I am suspicious of anyone who asks for commitments. I am especially hesitant when the claim demands urgency. There is plenty of time.

My commitment for "God's Word in My World" from our last session is:

ASSIGNMENT

Why did we break an assignment midchapter? Because Luke 9:51 begins a major theme in Luke's Gospel—the journey toward suffering. Jesus "determined to go to Jerusalem." The Savior continually reinterpreted Messiah. He carefully taught the lifestyle of the Kingdom. Listen as Jesus makes clear the cost of discipleship. Observe him explaining vulnerability that brings joy.

SPIRITUAL DISCIPLINES

Submission

We let go of our need always to be in control and make ourselves both available and vulnerable in commitment to others.

What would be different about today if I let go of my need to be in control?

How will I practice this discipline this week?

Sabbath

Sabbath calls us from the values of the culture that surrounds us to the values of the Kingdom. Culture puts self first; Kingdom puts others first.

Prayer

Pray daily before study:

"Whenever I'm afraid,
    I put my trust in you—
        in God, whose word I praise.
    I trust in God; I won't be afraid.
    What can mere flesh do to me?"
                        (Psalm 56:3-4).

Prayer concerns for the week:

Day 1 **Read Luke 9:51–10:24** (the cost of discipleship, mission of the seventy/seventy-two).

Day 2 **Read Luke 10:25-37** (the neighbor).

Day 3 **Read Luke 10:38–11:26** (Martha and Mary, the loving Father, Jesus and demons).

Day 4 **Read Luke 11:27–12:34** (woe to scribes and Pharisees).

Day 5 **Read Luke 12:35–13:35** (be ready, bear fruit, Sabbath healing, Jerusalem).

Day 6 **Read "Into the Word" and "Into the World" and answer the questions or provide responses.**

Day 7 **Rest, pray, and attend class.**

DISCIPLE FAST TRACK

INTO THE WORD

Temple was the focal point of Jerusalem. Jesus, a "shoot . . . from the stump of Jesse" (Isaiah 11:1), came out of Israel's life story and lifeblood. "It's impossible for a prophet to be killed outside of Jerusalem," he said (Luke 13:33).

Beginning with 9:51 Jesus literally "determined to go to Jerusalem." But it was not yet a geographical journey; it was a spiritual one. It did not matter to Luke that subsequent chapters show Jesus in Galilee, in Samaria, in Judea, even back and forth. Jesus, no matter where he put his feet, was drawn inexorably toward Jerusalem. Every step of the circuitous way, Jesus explained again and again he was pointed toward suffering (9:22).

Discipleship

Can a person join up with Jesus? Yes, but the cost is high. Many are unwilling to pay the price. "I will follow you wherever you go," said one. "The Human One has no place to lay his head," replied Jesus; and the man disappeared (Luke 9:57-58). Jesus invited another. That one called Jesus "Lord" but then begged off: "First let me go and bury my father" (9:59). The man meant, "Let me stay home with my father as long as he lives. Then when he is gone and all affairs are settled, then I will follow you." When Jesus spoke, he spoke in the now. The urgency of the Kingdom superseded everything else. "Let the dead bury their own dead" (9:60).

That is, let those who are dying, caught up in all the daily affairs that lead to decay and death, let them perform the burials. "But you go and spread the news of God's kingdom" (9:60).

Still another man declined, wanting to "first . . . say good-bye to those in my house" (9:61). For a son to leave his family, he must secure permission. The reluctant follower meant, "Let me go and see if it is all right, gain my father's blessing, and then come back to be a disciple." Jesus insisted that the call of the Kingdom takes precedence over the claims of family. In the presence of his own mother, Jesus said, "My mother and brothers are those who listen to God's word and do it" (8:21). God is God, so Jesus made the message unbelievably forceful and unmistakably clear. "Whoever comes to me and doesn't hate father and mother, spouse and children, and brothers and sisters—yes, even one's own life—cannot be my disciple" (14:26). Yes, hate. Here *hate* means "love less." For dramatic effect, he made clear that family must not hold us back from God's kingdom.

In what ways are you giving the Kingdom priority over family in your life?

Nor dare we waver or hesitate. When the call of salvation comes, the disciple dare not glance backward. "No one who puts a hand on the plow and looks back is fit for God's kingdom" (9:62). A kingdom had a king or queen to rule as an absolute sovereign. The kingdom of God is the realm of God's total and complete rule. To live in the kingdom of God is to give perfect allegiance to God's sovereignty. Jesus, as Son, calls us to discipleship, which is in fact a call to full participation in the kingdom of God.

But doesn't God govern the world? No, not in a full sense. Women and men in their freedom have rebelled against God. We often do what we please. Sins of all description alienate people from God. In fact, Jesus often intimated that Satan rules over sin, sickness, suffering, and death, and that the Son of Man came to break that powerful hold. So the issue is one of allegiance, of authority. Whose side are you on? When Jesus offers new life, he offers it in a new kingdom now breaking in upon us. The choice is open. God does not coerce. But the issue is life or death, God or Satan. The time is now.

The Good Neighbor

Luke is the only Gospel writer who records the story of the man who was the neighbor (Luke 10:25-37). It is one of the church's favorites because it is such a perfect story. But it would not be a favorite if we understood it; we would despise it, even as Jesus' listeners despised it.

Our problem is we do not fully comprehend the hatred between Jews and Samaritans. The mutual contempt between Samaritans and Jews was inexpressible. The Samaritans were Israelites, some of whom had intermarried with foreigners after Israel was overrun by the Assyrians. They worshiped at Mount Gerizim, not in Jerusalem. They read only the Pentateuch, not the Prophets or the Writings. They lived in an area on the west side of the Jordan River, south of Galilee, north of Jerusalem.

Jews traveling from Jerusalem to Galilee would first go east, cross over the Jordan, and walk north, considerably out of their way, to avoid passing through Samaria, partly out of hatred, partly out of fear. In Luke 9:51-56 we discover that, in spite of his fame as healer, teacher, and friend to all, when Jesus sent messengers to see if he would be welcome in a certain Samaritan village, he was refused.

So now, look at the "good Samaritan" story, word for word. Don't remove the parable from the debate around it, for the dialogue between Jesus and the lawyer provides the essential context for our understanding. The words *lawyer*, *scribe*, and *legal expert* refer to the same group: well-educated Jewish laymen, students of the Law, and proficient in deciding the intricate variations of Jewish law.

The lawyer "stood up" (10:25), a mark of respect, and said, "Teacher," also respectful but without the flattery of the rich ruler who asked the same question in 18:18-19. "What must I do to gain eternal life?" (10:25). Jesus could have responded in one of two ways. Much of the Old Testament teaches that life is a gift from God. Israel's inheritance is God's gracious gift. That would be like

Christians saying we are saved by grace. But the other strain of Hebrew thought strongly developed in rabbinical teachings was that to keep the Law was to live in God's favor. This truth also was well grounded in the Old Testament. The man asking the question was a lawyer. Jesus would deal with him on his own terms. The man was not seeking salvation for himself; he was probing to discover Jesus' idea about the Law. He wanted to test Jesus' loyalty.

So Jesus put the question back to the lawyer. "What is written in the Law? How do *you* interpret it?" (10:26, emphasis added). The law meant all that was written in the Pentateuch plus the oral tradition of interpretation. What would be a core answer? In Deuteronomy 6:5, the command is to love God. In Leviticus 19:18, the command is to love neighbor. When the lawyer replied with these texts (Luke 10:27), Jesus complimented him. The man had good theology. Was he willing to act upon it?

But the problem for a legalist is definition. This man wanted to *do* several things and be righteous. Compare again the rich ruler in Luke 18:18-23. The only way to be a successful moralist—Jewish, Christian, or otherwise—is to have a list of rules, a group of *do's* and *don'ts* and then to keep them.

So the lawyer, seeking to "prove that he was right" (10:29), that is, be able to do certain things or refrain from doing certain things in order to stand righteous before God, pressed the debate further. "And who is my neighbor?" The rabbis had spent generations discussing that point. Family, yes. Jewish associates, yes, under most circumstances. Proselytes, probably not. Sinners, Gentiles, outsiders, no. People being punished by God? Never. The man wanted Jesus to define a group of neighbors, to say, "Your family and those who live in your neighborhood." He wanted a limited definition.

So Jesus told a story. Every listener knew that the road from Jerusalem to Jericho was a dangerous, treacherous seventeen miles, starting at 2300 feet above sea level and weaving its narrow way down through the Wadi Qelt toward the Jordan River. The path wound around barren rock slides, down steep slopes, past huge boulders where thieves and murderers often hid in waiting.

The man was presumed Jewish, although Jesus did not identify him. Robbers struck him down, beat him nearly to death, took everything he had, even stripped him naked, and then dumped him beside the road—a somewhat common occurrence.

A priest also was going down, presumably on a donkey, for a priest had financial means and status. The sight of the limp body set his religious mind racing. If the man were a good Jew and alive, he should help him. If on the other hand, he were a sinner being struck down by God, or a Gentile, he should not. He remembered a law that said he should assist a Jew being beaten by robbers, but it was too late for that.

Was the man alive or dead? The priest did not know. If he got closer than four cubits (six feet) to a corpse, he would be defiled. He would have to turn around, go back to Jerusalem, undergo a week's ceremonial purification at considerable expense and effort. He could not serve as priest until he did those things. Struggling to be a good man, the priest was paralyzed. He and his donkey passed on by.

The Levite had the same set of problems if the man were dead. If alive, the body could be contaminated, infected. The robbers could still be in the vicinity. One hesitation and two bodies might lie in the ditch. Besides, on a road like that, pilgrims usually knew who was traveling. They asked questions. If he knew that the priest was ahead of him, then he also knew that the moral leader, zealous in keeping the Law, had ignored the body. To act counter to the priest would be criticizing the priest's decision. The Levite may have been asking, "What good could I do?" He did take a closer look. What sort of man lay there?

In Jesus' day especially, though still today, ethnic religious communities are distinct. You knew who people were in one of two ways, their dress or their speech. At a distance you could recognize a Jew, a Greek, a Roman, a Samaritan. Ask a question or two, and you could detect the speech of a particular region. People often knew which village a person came from. The naked man in the ditch was silent. In that moment he belonged to no religious or ethnic community. He was neighbor to no one and everyone. The Levite also passed by.

Now the listeners were ready for a Jewish layman to appear. It was the natural order of the three categories of Jews—priests, Levites, and laymen.

But the third man was a hated Samaritan.

The priest had passed by. The Levite came to the place but also passed by. The Samaritan "came to where the man was" (10:33). He, too, risked contamination. He, too, was vulnerable to robbers, more perhaps than the respected priest or Levite. If the wounded man were a Jew, the Samaritan might risk retaliation from family for taking the man to the inn.

Bandaging wounds is the imagery used of God in saving the covenant people: "I will heal your wounds" (Jeremiah 30:17). Wine and oil not only were antiseptic and healing but were also the libations poured out in the Temple by priests and Levites. The Samaritan put the man on his own riding animal, while he walked leading the animal.

At the inn he stayed all night, nursing the man. On departure the next day, he left two denarii, two days' wages for a laboring man. The innkeeper could have had the injured man arrested if he could not pay the bill. What the robbers took, the Samaritan provided.

Then Jesus asked, "Which one of these three was a neighbor?" (Luke 10:36). Notice that Jesus changed the focus of the original question from "Who is my neighbor?" to "Who acted neighborly?"—a critical change. The lawyer replied, "The one who demonstrated mercy toward him" (10:37). "Go," said Jesus, "and do likewise."

DISCIPLE FAST TRACK

The early church quickly observed that the "good Samaritan," in his compassionate vulnerability and love, looked greatly like Jesus on his way to Jerusalem. The lawyer was standing closer to the "good Samaritan" than he knew.

Choosing the Better Part

Martha, Mary, and Lazarus lived in the tiny village of Bethany, on the lower eastern slope of the Mount of Olives, about two miles east of Jerusalem. Two sisters and a brother living together, the three had become some of Jesus' closest friends. No home brought him more joy to visit. John's Gospel records the raising of Lazarus from the tomb. Only Luke tells the story of Martha and Mary offering hospitality to Jesus (Luke 10:38-42). The scene is so human, so familiar to every household.

Martha was a "take charge" person. She took charge when Lazarus died, sending urgently for Jesus. She now was preparing a meal for Jesus. With all the work to be done, where was Mary, her sister? She was sitting right at Jesus' feet, listening intently "to his message" (10:39).

Martha was overburdened. We can appreciate her. She is the one we count on when we are hungry. Notice her salutation to Jesus. She called him "Lord" but was completely familiar. "Don't you care that my sister has left me to prepare the table all by myself? Tell her to help me" (10:40).

Emotionally Jesus was on his way to Jerusalem. He needed friendship more than food. Mary, whose Lord would not be with her much longer, needed his words more than supper.

"Martha, Martha, you are worried and distracted. . . . One thing is necessary" (10:41-42). Mary chose the better part, for "people don't live on bread alone. No, they live based on whatever the LORD says" (Deuteronomy 8:3).

Be Ready

At least three meanings are included in the phrase *kingdom of God* or *kingdom of heaven*. The first meaning is the immediate experience with Jesus. Jesus came preaching the Kingdom. To confront Jesus was and is to confront the claims of the kingdom of God. "Now is the time! Here comes God's kingdom! Change your hearts and lives, and trust this good news!" (Mark 1:15).

When the seventy* returned with joy, they reported, "Lord, even the demons submit themselves to us in your name" (Luke 10:17). Jesus responded, "I saw Satan fall from heaven like lightning" (10:18). People were being touched by the rule of God.

After one amazing healing, someone said, "He throws out demons with the authority of Beelzebul," that is, the devil (11:15). No! Someone stronger has broken into Beelzebul's kingdom. "But if I throw out demons by the power of God, then God's kingdom has already overtaken you" (11:20).

The second meaning has to do with God's judgment. God's judgment can come at any time, for a person, a city, a nation. We must not be careless or indifferent. Jesus wept over Jerusalem

* Other ancient authorities say "seventy-two."

(19:41), for he knew that the forces of destruction were already brewing. Within a few years the Temple would be destroyed (A.D. 70), never to be rebuilt. "Jerusalem, Jerusalem . . . How often I have wanted to gather your people just as a hen gathers her chicks under her wings. But you didn't want that" (13:34).

God's rule cuts two ways. It brings judgment to those who are not ready, salvation to those who are prepared.

The third meaning concerns the culmination of history, when God draws the curtain on the final act. You will see the Human One coming in his glory, and all the angels with him (Matthew 25:31), often called the Second Coming. Jesus pleaded with his disciples to keep watch and always be ready. Read carefully Luke 12:35-48. A servant pulls up his long robe, tucks it into his belt so he can be busy about his work. The wick in the oil lamps must be kept trimmed, for who knows when the bridegroom will arrive? Be ready. Be engaged in Kingdom business, "because the Human One is coming at a time when you don't expect him" (12:40).

How does each of these meanings of Kingdom influence your daily life?

INTO THE WORLD

Before we give, we must receive. Before we go on a spiritual journey, we have to have a place to stand. That is why Jesus insisted that the center of our souls can be filled with that spark of affection called the Holy Spirit. Before you go into the world, invite the Spirit of Jesus Christ to take authority and reside within you.

This week we consider the cost of discipleship. God's kingdom is available to the obedient and the vulnerable.

Try changing some priorities. Most of us protect our daily patterns so that we never see a woman who is abused, a baby addicted to drugs, a family who is homeless. What could we do to break our complacent rhythm of insulated self-protection?

Here are suggestions of ways to sensitize your spirit:

• Go to a hospital emergency room and sit for one hour. Visit with someone who is waiting.
• Try riding in a police car for an evening.
• Help one evening at a rescue mission or Salvation Army shelter. Take some food or clothes. Stay for supper and visit with people.

Why do these activities seem strange? Jesus seemed to gravitate to human pain. We try to separate ourselves from it. Our hearts slowly harden until we no longer see or hear the hurt. Sometimes, if we get close enough, we will find a ministry that will launch us into a whole new excitement.

God's Word in My World
In what new ways will this session's message from God's Word influence my daily thoughts, attitudes, and actions so I continue to become more like Christ?

I will commit to integrating the above response into my daily living beginning this week by following this specific, measurable action:

IF YOU WANT TO KNOW MORE

Matthew has many parables that begin "The kingdom of heaven is like . . ." To broaden your understanding of Kingdom, read Matthew 13:44-50; 18:23-35; 20:1-16.

"All who exalt themselves will be humbled, but all who humble themselves will be exalted."
—Luke 18:14, NRSV

5 Learning to Follow

OUR HUMAN CONDITION

Humility sounds weak, spineless. In an attempt to be humble, we become condescending. So many of our role models are aggressive, self-centered. We don't know how to be humble and still be strong and radiant.

My commitment for "God's Word in My World" from our last session is:

ASSIGNMENT

Jesus told parable after parable about the Kingdom. Listen on several levels. Read like the crowd, happy to hear a good story. Read like the disciples, eager to understand the kernel of meaning. Read in the light of the Crucifixion and the Resurrection to discover spiritual guidance for your life.

SPIRITUAL DISCIPLINES

Simplicity
As we come to see money not as our security but as a trust from God, we will use it joyfully in behalf of others.

If today I see myself as a steward of God's money rather than an owner of money, how will I spend it differently?

How will I practice this discipline this week?

Sabbath
In ceasing work for one day, we are free to see ourselves in the image of God rather than define ourselves by what we produce and consume. We give up our need to compete, our drive toward efficiency, our striving to achieve. We accept God's gifts of rest, dignity, peace, freedom.

Prayer
Pray daily before study:

"Not to us, LORD, not to us—
  no, but to your own name give glory
    because of your loyal love and faithfulness!"
(Psalm 115:1).

Prayer concerns for the week:

Day 1 **Read Luke 14:25-35; 15** (estimate the cost, the search for the lost).

Day 2 **Read Luke 16** (money: the shrewd manager, the rich man and Lazarus).

Day 3 **Read Luke 17** (sin, faith, gratitude, preparedness).

Day 4 **Read Luke 18** (the persistent widow, Pharisee and tax collector, the rich ruler, Jesus' suffering foretold).

Day 5 **Read Luke 19:1-27** (Zacchaeus, ten pounds); **Matthew 25:14-46** (talents, Great Judgment).

Day 6 **Read "Into the Word" and "Into the World" and answer the questions or provide responses.**

Day 7 **Rest, pray, and attend class.**

INTO THE WORD

As Jesus moved close to his suffering, he reminded people that discipleship demands a price. A student is not above the teacher. If the teacher walks toward the cross, disciples must "take up their cross daily, and follow me" (Luke 9:23).

The tower (14:28-30), probably a vineyard tower, was built so the owner could keep watch for thieves during harvest. An unfinished building is always a humiliation to its builder. Every builder must first ask, "How much will it cost?"

Wars were commonplace, one king against another. Jesus probably had a specific war in mind (14:31-33). A king with a small army might decide to pay a large tribute rather than be destroyed. What are the terms of discipleship?

Salt is distinctive (14:34-35). In the ancient world, salt was expensive. Salt crystals were found in rock formations. The whole aggregate was crushed, and either in the preparation of the meal or at the table, people would pick out the clumps of salt crystals. Finally the picked-over residue, fit for nothing, was thrown out. If you are going to be a disciple, either you will be perceptibly peculiar or worthless.

Searching for the Lost

You will not understand the three stories of lostness—lost sheep, lost coin, and lost son—if you miss Luke's context for them (Luke 15:1-2). Religious leaders were grumbling. What was the problem? Jesus was eating with sinners, some immoral and some ceremonially unclean. The law-abiding leaders gave food to the poor, attention to the injured, care to the destitute, of course; but they didn't give them table fellowship. That implied community, precisely what the Pharisees avoided and what Jesus extended. "This man welcomes sinners" (15:2). A better translation might be "receives" them (RSV), for Jesus was hosting the meal. What is the first word spoken by a Near Eastern host? "You have honored me; you have honored my house by coming to my lowly dinner." The tax collector, the woman of the evening, the Samaritan, the day laborer—all were honoring Jesus by eating at his meal? What is going on?

Now the stories.

"Suppose someone among you had one hundred sheep . . . ?" (15:4). Right off he humbled the professionals. Sheep were tended by peasants. No educated, cultured persons, no persons of status, would be caught dead working with sheep.

There were two kinds of shepherds: bedouin and village shepherds. The image is more one of village people. Each family would own five or ten sheep, maybe twenty. The extended family, including uncles and cousins, perhaps neighbors, would put together a flock of a hundred sheep. They would then pay two or three in the family, even children, to look after the flock. One person would not be a shepherd alone.

One of the shepherds, after a head count in the wilderness, went in search of the lost sheep. One sheep, like one person, is important. The *search* is a common theme in the three stories. A shepherd, listening, would smile wryly at the word *rejoice,* for what has the shepherd found? A wounded sheep, a sick sheep, a stubborn sheep, lying exhausted in the rocks? It's impossible to drive one sheep home, sick or well. The work has just begun. The search was only half the cost. The shepherd would pick up the animal, lay it across his shoulders legs forward, grab two feet with each hand, and walk the long way home.

The ninety-nine were brought back to the village at evening by the other shepherds. It was dangerous for one person, perhaps a woman or a child, to go searching alone. The people of the village at dusk had an eye out. Now the shepherd comes home. The sheep, a part of community property, is recovered. It is time for a second rejoicing, a community rejoicing. Can you imagine somebody unhappy over the return of the sheep? Yet the Pharisees and scribes were precisely that; they were glum because Jesus brought "lost" people back to God. He brought people who were apart back into community.

The second story (15:8-10) highlights a woman as heroine, unusual in that culture. A bedouin woman would have her dowry of ten silver coins on an ornamental chain around her head or neck. A village woman would have her coins tied tightly in a handkerchief. Cash money in a village was in short supply. Food they grew. Clothing they made. Money, little as it was, they saved.

At least she knew where the coin was; it was in the house somewhere. She looked in the corners for the tenth time. She moved the bedding, swept up every bit of dust, until she found the coin. Note the commitment and intensity of the search. Overcome with joy, she called the neighbors. The angels rejoice over one sinner who repents.

Only Luke offers us the story of the lost son, or better, the compassionate father (15:11-32). The older son would inherit two thirds of the father's property, and the younger son one third when the father died. The younger son wanted his now, an unheard-of request. To demand inheritance in effect said, "Father, I wish you were dead." Even property given could not be sold without the father's consent. The father gave it, much to the consternation of friends and relatives and to the shame of the family. The son took the money into a distant country and squandered it in "extravagant living" (15:13). Hard times came, a famine. Lots of men were looking for work. The son hired out to do the lowest task a Jew could perform, feeding pigs. He would even have eaten "what the pigs ate" if it had been offered. He rehearsed his speech in which he would apologize to his father and ask to be a hired hand. That would be a lowly job but independent. He might be able to pay his father back, and he would not have to eat at his brother's table. He still could not see the critical issue—the relationship he had broken with his father.

The father spent a lot of time scanning the horizon. When he saw the son "still a long way off" (15:20), he began to run. No man over thirty runs in Palestine. Boys run. Men learn to walk slowly, with dignity and honor, letting their long robes cover their feet. Picture the father, grabbing his robe, pulling it above his knees, running breathlessly through the streets of the village. Neighbors would be gasping, little boys running after him. Picture him. Kissing the son first on one cheek, then on the other, not letting him recite his speech. He called for a robe (the best one would be his own), a ring (authority over property matters), and sandals. Slaves and servants went barefoot; sons wore sandals. He called for the fatted calf, the one calf penned up to be grain-fed for a holiday.

The villagers had crossed him off, this prodigal. But what indifference to shame, ridicule, and derision the father showed; for he understood the real issue. Father and son were together. The son was alive again.

Some think another parable follows, but not so. The one parable is not finished, for the whole point is restoration into community by a compassionate father. The older son was sulking, would not come into the house, bad-mouthed his brother, claiming he had devoured the money "on prostitutes" (15:30), something the story had not said. He called him "this son of yours," refusing to say "my brother." He felt sorry for himself, working steadily, staying at home. No humility or compassion in *his* heart.

Now the father, while the guests stood amazed at his loss of dignity, went outside and pleaded with the older son, not on the basis of money but on the basis of family, "Son, you are always with me"—an affirmation instead of a reproof. "Everything I have is yours." He had divided the property earlier. "This brother of yours"—that's the issue. The father was willing to pay the costly price of reconciliation. "This brother of yours."

The question left is whether the older brother was also willing to pay that same price so that the family could be together again.

What do you think was going through the minds of the listeners as Jesus told these three parables?

The Shrewd Manager

We find this parable (Luke 16:1-13) difficult, not because we can't comprehend the story but because we don't understand the meaning. We are surprised that Jesus used a rascal to make a point. True, Jesus used the ordinary stuff of everyday life for illustrations. He has presented less-than-admirable characters before—the uncaring judge and a friend who didn't want to be bothered. But this manager, who had been either skimming or sloppy, ended up being praised by his boss and by Jesus.

NOTES

The rich man of the village owned several farms, so he had an estate manager to negotiate contracts and look after things. The renters agreed to cash rent, that is, so much olive oil and so much wheat, no matter how well the crops turned out. The amounts would be paid when the crops were harvested.

The owner called his manager into his office and fired him for "wasting his estate" (16:1). "Give me a report of your administration because you can no longer serve as my manager" (16:2). Commentators note that the owner did not put the manager in jail, nor did he curse or berate him. He simply let him go. The manager, by his silence, indicated his guilt.

But then the manager came face-to-face with his future. Moments before, he had position, a certain power, adequate income. Now he suddenly felt old, too old for day labor, too proud to beg. He was powerless, a man without authority, without a job. He would receive no favorable recommendations. He was at the end of his tether: no job, no friends, no future.

Like a flash, he had a clever idea. Quickly he called the renters to him. Contracts had been renegotiated before when it did not rain, when insects devoured the crop, usually at the renters' request. The renters, now, were both dumbfounded and elated. The manager said, "Take your contract and, instead of nine hundred jugs of olive oil rent due at harvest, write four hundred fifty jugs." Again, to another, "Instead of one thousand bushels of wheat rent due at harvest, write eight hundred." Both signed, the renters assuming the owner knew about and approved the action. The manager may very well have hinted that he had urged the owner to relax the rent for them. The renters thought he was wonderful. He was their friend. "Come eat with us sometime."

Probably within hours the whole village knew about the action, not as fraud but as generosity. When the manager brought in the records, the owner already had heard his name being praised. The owner had two choices: He could try to undo the action and make everyone in the village angry with him, or he could let it go so that the renters would continue to praise him and appreciate the manager.

He chose to let the reduced contracts stand. That was what the manager was counting on. In the back of his mind, the manager knew he had one source of salvation, the good will of those whose rent he had reduced.

The owner and Jesus praised the manager. For what? For being shrewd in an emergency, for looking out for his welfare. People spend time and money planning their financial future. If only they were as perceptive in figuring out their eternal future.

The shrewd manager was praised, not because he was crooked but because he put his mind to work on his future destiny and because he trusted in the goodwill of those he had aided. Jesus said "people who belong to the light" should be so shrewd (16:8), use wealth to secure an eternal home (16:9). We do not buy a place in heaven, but secure a place by thoughtful generosity and kindness to those in need.

Children

Jesus pointed to children as examples of the Kingdom. Look at these teachings:

- "God's kingdom belongs to people like these children" (Luke 18:16).
- "Whoever doesn't welcome God's kingdom like a child will never enter it" (18:17).
- The disciples asked Jesus, "Who is the greatest in the kingdom of heaven?" (Matthew 18:1). He put a child on his lap and taught, "If you don't turn your lives around and become like this little child, you will definitely not enter the kingdom of heaven" (18:3).
- Who are the greatest? Again he took a child and said, "Whoever is least among you all is the greatest" (Luke 9:46-48).
- Here is a powerful teaching: "Whoever welcomes one such child in my name welcomes me" (Matthew 18:5). If we can help a child, we help Jesus. See also Matthew 25:35-40 and apply that passage to treatment of children. What is the judgment of this passage on our society?

- To cause another person to sin is a grievous act. But to cause a child to sin—listen to this: "As for whoever causes these little ones who believe in me to trip and fall into sin, it would be better for them to have a huge stone hung around their necks and be drowned in the bottom of the lake" (18:6). This teaching might cause conscientious parents to feel guilty. Yet terrible crimes are committed against children that drive them to sinful ways. What stumbling blocks are we putting before our children?

What Is a Servant to Do?

Everyone loves a story about a celebrity, a rich man about to be made king (Luke 19:12). Suspense is introduced when he gives ten servants each a gold coin and says, "See what you can earn with this while I am gone" (19:13, GNT). Already we know the rich man was hated (19:14). Later he acknowledged that he was "a hard man, taking what is not mine and reaping what I have not planted" (19:22, GNT). The man wanted results.

NOTES

We would like to hire the first man as an investment counselor, although we have no idea how he made ten gold coins out of the one. He said he "earned" it (19:16, GNT). With a "well done," the rich man, now king, put him in charge of ten cities.

The second man earned five gold coins (19:18, GNT). He did not receive a "well done" but was placed over five cities.

The third man is pivotal. He made two mistakes. He misjudged his king, and he was unproductive. He should have acted bravely according to the expectations of the king. He knew the kind of man he served. Even timidly he could have put the money in the bank and earned some meager interest.

Now comes the part of the story so seemingly harsh, even to those standing by: "Take his money and give it to the one who has ten times as much" (19:24). The act seems doubly unfair. It takes from the one with little and gives to the most prosperous. Why not at least make it a little more even by giving it to the man with five? But no! "Everyone who has will be given more" (19:26).

What is the one basic teaching in this parable? Matthew's Gospel helps us, because it follows up the parable (Matthew 25:14-30) with a judgment scene (25:31-46). In the judgment as in the parable, some are rewarded and some severely punished. What was the king looking for? Risk. Productivity. Stewardship of time, energy, talent.

But doing what? That's the point. It is important to know for whom you are working. What did the king expect? In the parable, the king wanted money, lots of it. In the judgment scene of Matthew 25, the king wants the hungry to be fed, the thirsty to be given drink, the stranger to be received, the naked to be clothed, the sick to be cared for, the prisoner to be visited (25:34-40).

Jesus said, "Not everybody who says to me, 'Lord, Lord,' will get into the kingdom of heaven. Only those who do the will of my Father who is in heaven will enter" (Matthew 7:21). The third servant said, "Lord, Lord," but failed to do the will of his king.

INTO THE WORLD

Usually we think of evangelism as witness leading to conversion and profession of faith. Think this week of evangelism as table fellowship. Try to eat with someone who needs to experience inclusiveness and community. How can you show genuine interest rather than obligation? How can you be sure your actions express a humble rather than a condescending spirit?

DISCIPLE FAST TRACK

One emphasis from our Scripture study has been on children. What are the needs of our children in today's world?

What could your group do to assist community efforts for immunization? Could your church set up a free clinic?

Some towns have a "coat drive," sponsored by schools, radio stations, and dry cleaners, to obtain a warm coat for every child. A volunteer group usually works with schoolteachers. Do you have such a plan, or might you start one?

Does your church have an after-school program for children? Or a counseling ministry for potential school dropouts?

How well supplied is your church's food pantry where families with children can obtain emergency foodstuffs? Could you check to see how adequate it is?

God's Word in My World

In what new ways will this session's message from God's Word influence my daily thoughts, attitudes, and actions so I continue to become more like Christ?

I will commit to integrating the above response into my daily living beginning this week by following this specific, measurable action:

IF YOU WANT TO KNOW MORE

We often read about Samaritans in Luke's Gospel. Read John 4:1-42. If this experience was the introduction of the gospel into Samaria, think of the absolute humility and vulnerability of Jesus. Think of the slow yet significant opening of the woman to Jesus' words. Realize who it was that became the first evangelist-missionary to the Samaritans.

NOTES

"Repentance and forgiveness of sins is to be proclaimed in his name to all nations, beginning from Jerusalem. You are witnesses of these things."
—Luke 24:47-48, NRSV

6 Sent as Witnesses

OUR HUMAN CONDITION

We can be witnesses only to what we have experienced. Being a witness for an unpopular cause or an idea that runs counter to the culture can be intimidating, humiliating, even dangerous. And inconvenient.

My commitment for "God's Word in My World" from our last session is:

ASSIGNMENT

We call the suffering of Jesus—arrest, trial, crucifixion, burial—the Passion. Each of the four Gospel writers provides a "Passion portrait," and each reports Christ's victory over death in the Resurrection. Luke uniquely includes many teachings in the Temple. Luke also emphasizes the human side of Jesus' obedience. Read the account slowly, for everything in the Bible prior to these events is merely prelude; everything after is commentary on the mighty act of God in Christ.

SPIRITUAL DISCIPLINES

Prayer

An awareness of God's continuing presence creates in us an attitude of praying without ceasing.

How do I learn to pray without ceasing so that I am listening to God without ceasing?

How will I practice this discipline this week?

Sabbath

Sabbath offers a balanced and hopeful view of life. It does not deny the pain, the sorrow, the sadness. Rather, it breaks into the pain and sadness with a time of joy, fellowship, intimacy, and renewal.

Prayer

Pray daily before study:

"Return the joy of your salvation to me
and sustain me with a willing spirit.
Then I will teach wrongdoers your ways,
and sinners will come back to you"
(Psalm 51:12-13).

Prayer concerns for the week:

Day 1 Read Luke 19:28-48 (Palm Sunday).

Day 4 Read Luke 23 (Crucifixion and burial).

Day 2 Read Luke 20–21 (teaching in the Temple).

Day 5 Read Luke 24 (Resurrection and empty tomb, Emmaus road, the great command).

Day 3 Read Luke 22 (betrayal, Passover meal, the garden, arrest, and trial).

Day 6 Read "Into the Word" and "Into the World" and answer the questions or provide responses.

Day 7 Rest, pray, and attend class.

INTO THE WORD

The crucifixion and resurrection of Jesus was the message proclaimed by the early church and the heart of early church preaching. Each of the four Gospels records the arrest, trial, crucifixion, and resurrection of Jesus. The accounts vary in detail, but the central events were reported fundamentally the same, amazingly so. The community of faith told the story over and over again until some people began to write it down.

Luke brings to us the witness of the early church. So let us approach our study of Jesus' suffering, death, and resurrection by asking what the witnesses were saying to their world (and to us).

Confrontation

For Luke, Jesus had been moving toward Jerusalem throughout his ministry. Now he actually walked the path down from the Mount of Olives. The donkey colt was essential, not only to fulfill Zechariah's prophecy (Zechariah 9:9) but also to show Jesus' peaceful messiahship. When the two disciples untied the colt, saying, "Its master needs it" (Luke 19:34), the owners knew it was for Jesus and lent it gladly.

The sun in early morning turns the limestone buildings to pure gold. Facing Jerusalem from the top of the Mount of Olives, Jesus saw the city, not full of sunshine but full of hospitality, fear, greed, and intrigue; and he wept. "If only you knew . . . the things that lead to peace. . . . The time will come when your enemies will . . . attack you from all sides. They will crush you completely. . . . They won't leave one stone on top of another within you, because you didn't recognize the time of your gracious visit from God" (19:41-44).

What is the witness of the early church saying to us? Repent and accept grace while you can; the time quickly comes when it is too late. Jerusalem did not respond. Because of Jewish desire for independence, rebellion and fighting broke out periodically until in A.D. 70 the Roman legions leveled the city, desecrating and destroying the Temple. In A.D. 135 the cruel destruction was even worse. Romans totally sacked the city and prohibited all Jews, including Christians, from living there.

Why did Jesus cleanse the Temple? The money changers were exchanging Roman coins for Jewish money, suitable for paying the Temple tax. But were they honoring God? No, economic gain was being placed above worship. The traffic in the Temple laid the groundwork for corruption, not for worship, integrity, and peace.

What a contrast when Jesus spotted a poor widow putting two copper coins in the offering box. She gave all that she had (21:1-4). Her faith was the real thing. Infused into the power structure, it could have saved Jerusalem.

Luke's witness warns that troubles will come to the disciples as they did to Jesus. Early in his ministry Jesus taught, "Happy are you when people hate you, reject you, insult you, and condemn your name as evil because of the Human One. Rejoice. . . . Their ancestors did the same things to the prophets" (6:22-23). Now in Jerusalem, for Jesus and the disciples, the storm clouds gathered. Some terrible persecutions occurred even before these words were written down; others followed. "They will take you into custody and harass you because of your faith. They will hand you over to synagogues and prisons, and you will be brought before kings and governors because of my name" (21:12).

For most of us, persecution is nonexistent or extremely mild. Yet in many countries Christians are being tortured and killed for their faith. We would be surprised if we knew how many Christians lose a job because they refuse to perform an illegal action, how many people lose a love because they refuse an immoral relationship, how many people are excluded because they are unwilling to go with the crowd.

We are not left without counsel. Whenever we are excluded or defamed, that moment will provide for us "an opportunity to testify" (21:13). Jesus tells us not to worry about what we should say, he will give us the words to speak (21:15).

Resistance

Resistance to Jesus intensified as his popularity increased. The Passover pilgrims flocked to Jerusalem. Crowds thronged to listen to Jesus teach in the Temple. Embarrassed at Jesus' popularity, fearful of his growing power, the religious leaders "were looking for a way to kill Jesus" (Luke 22:2).

Judas

Judas confuses us, perplexes us now as he did others then. What had gone wrong? Did not Jesus pray all night before he chose Judas? Did Judas become disillusioned when Messiah walked the road to suffering? Did he try to force Jesus' hand, try to turn him into a political revolutionary? When did Judas first allow Satan to control his mind? We cannot tell, but we observe the awful finality as "Satan entered Judas" (Luke 22:3).

Luke saved his description of Judas's death for Acts 1:15-20 when Peter led the faithful to select someone to take Judas's place. Judas became for us a negative witness.

The witnesses wanted us to know that evil's power always stands ready. Satan can enter into our thoughts and actions. The battle of faithfulness is never finished. No wonder Jesus taught us to pray in the Lord's Prayer, "Rescue us from the evil one" (Matthew 6:13).

When have you known you were doing wrong yet did it anyway?

The Meal

The Seder, or Passover meal, was intensely important for Jesus. He had made preparations. The disciples would find a man carrying a jar of water. Normally a woman would carry water, so this was unusual. The man had the upstairs room completely furnished (Luke 22:10-12).

At the supper Jesus explained that his suffering would come soon. "I won't eat it until it is fulfilled in God's kingdom" (Luke 22:16). When the faithful are called from the east and the west, the north and the south, they will sit down at table with the Lord, breaking bread and drinking the cup (13:29).

The Lord commanded that we eat this bread and drink this cup. It is a part of our witness to his suffering, to our table fellowship, and to his coming again. Christians call this holy meal Eucharist (meaning "thanksgiving"); Holy Communion; the Lord's Supper; the Mass (meaning "to send"); the Sacrament (meaning "to consecrate"). We witness when we eat this meal together.

Suffering

The church from the beginning recalled the sufferings of Jesus. The spiritual sufferings were surely painful—the denial by Peter, the betrayal by Judas, the agony in the garden. But the physical torture was terrible. The soldiers who took him captive in the garden were not Roman soldiers; they were Temple police (Luke 22:52). They took their prisoner to the high priest's house (22:54). They blindfolded him, beat him, mocked him (22:63-65).

The sequence of trials in Luke's Gospel starts with a hearing before the Sanhedrin, although it seems to have been hastily called and therefore an illegal meeting with less than full representation (22:66). The charge was blasphemy, that Jesus had claimed divine authority. In Luke's Gospel Jesus had not used the phrase "God's Son," so the words were theirs (22:70-71).

Under Roman law Jewish authorities had some limited power but not the power of life and death. Capital punishment required Roman approval. So the Sanhedrin took Jesus to Pontius Pilate, the Roman governor in Jerusalem. The charges were these: perverting the nation, teaching people not to pay taxes to the emperor, and proclaiming himself a king (23:2).

In effect, these charges meant insurrection, civil disobedience, and treason. When Pilate said the accusations did not hold up, the accusers then argued, "He agitates the people" (23:5), also a serious charge, disturbing the peace. The Roman rulers allowed some things but not a riot that might erupt into a revolution.

When Pilate learned that Jesus was a Galilean, he sent him to Tetrarch Herod Antipas, who was in town for Passover and who governed Galilee. Herod, "that fox" (13:32), had wanted to see Jesus for a long time (9:7-9). Jesus stood silent before questions, ridicule, and mockings as if he were fulfilling Isaiah's prophecy: "Like a lamb being brought to slaughter, / like a ewe silent before her shearers, / he didn't open his mouth" (Isaiah 53:7).

Settling this dispute over jurisdiction caused Pilate and Herod to become friends (Luke 23:12). Pilate saw a chance to pass the buck; Herod took it as a recognition of *his* authority. Back to Pilate. Luke wanted his readers to know that neither Pilate nor Herod found any fault in Jesus. Luke also broadened his appeal to Gentiles: Jesus was innocent of treason or insurrection. But Pilate released Barabbas and turned Jesus over to Roman soldiers to be crucified.

When Jesus died, the sky turned dark, and the curtain in the Temple was torn (Luke 23:45). Matthew's Gospel says it was torn "from top to bottom" (Matthew 27:51). Do you remember when the curtain was first placed in the Tabernacle so that only Aaron could go behind it to stand before the ark and offer sacrifice once a year for atonement? Now God has torn down the curtain from heaven to earth, for the perfect Lamb has been offered.

Luke wanted us to know that Jesus in his humility was obedient to death. A Gentile, a Roman soldier, said "It's really true: this man was righteous" (Luke 23:47).

Witnesses to the Resurrection

Suppose Luke wanted to summarize the total ministry of the Human One, the Son of Man—man, message, cross, and tomb—in one episode. What event would he choose?

In his concluding chapter, between the accounts of the women and Peter at the empty tomb and Jesus' appearance to the disciples, Luke recorded the walk to Emmaus. The story is given to us only by Luke. Emmaus means "warm springs." Scholars debate its location. Two disciples were walking toward Emmaus, talking about all that had happened. The time was Easter afternoon. The place was a little way out of Jerusalem. Both men had been caught up in the Crucifixion event and had heard the women tell of the vision of angels at the empty tomb.

A stranger began to walk with them. So engrossed were they in their conversation that they didn't notice where he came from. As Jesus began to question them, they poured out their grief, their dashed hopes, their perplexity about the women's tales.

These disciples did not recognize Jesus! Neither had Israel. Neither had the world. Spiritual blindness caused them not to see. Luke wanted us to spot that, because the resurrected Jesus said to them, "You foolish people! Your dull minds keep you from believing all that the prophets talked about" (Luke 24:25).

In Luke's entire Gospel, Jesus was continually trying to interpret the Scripture for Israel. He tried to explain that their problem was not with him; they were in conflict with their own Scriptures! But even the disciples were not able to understand the meaning of Scripture until after the Crucifixion and the Resurrection.

How does your view of the Crucifixion and the Resurrection shape your understanding of Scripture?

DISCIPLE FAST TRACK

NOTES

Carefully Jesus traced scriptural meanings for them, "starting with Moses and going through all the Prophets" (24:27). Did Jesus quote Moses, "The LORD your God will raise up a prophet like me from your community, from your fellow Israelites" (Deuteronomy 18:15)? Did he refer to the sufferings of Jeremiah, whose tears for the people flowed like a spring of water (Jeremiah 9:1)? Did he mention the tenderness of Ezekiel, "I will appoint for them a single shepherd, and he will feed them" (Ezekiel 34:23)?

Surely Jesus quoted Isaiah: "He was pierced because of our rebellions / and crushed because of our crimes. / He bore the punishment that made us whole; / by his wounds we are healed" (Isaiah 53:5).

Luke wanted us to know that with Resurrection eyes we can understand the Scriptures. The way of God in the world is plain. "If they don't listen to Moses and the Prophets, then neither will they be persuaded if someone rises from the dead" (Luke 16:31). Why could they not recognize the stranger? Because faith is generated by a clear understanding of Scripture. That understanding comes after the Crucifixion and the Resurrection. Later, after Jesus had vanished, they said to each other, "Weren't our hearts on fire when he spoke to us along the road and when he explained the scriptures for us?" (24:32).

Evening came. They begged the stranger to stay and eat supper with them. Do you see it unfolding? Are you re-experiencing Abraham, entertaining "angels without knowing it" (Genesis 18:1-8; Hebrews 13:2)? Are you hearing, "I was hungry and you gave me food. . . . 'Lord, when did we see you hungry and feed you . . . ?' I assure you that when you have done it for one of the least of these brothers and sisters of mine . . ." (Matthew 25:35-40)? Most of all, for Luke's sake, are you ready to absorb the spiritual power of table fellowship? "After he took his seat at the table with them, he took the bread, blessed and broke it, and gave it to them. Their eyes were opened and they recognized him" (Luke 24:30-31).

Jesus vanished from their sight. But even though it was evening, they hurried back to Jerusalem and found the eleven and other friends. Luke wanted us to know for certain that people of faith, people who have encountered the risen Lord, are *witnesses*. Already the Book of Acts is on the tip of his pen. The two discouraged disciples were now aglow. They told the story. That's what disciples are supposed to do. They explained "how Jesus was made known to them as he broke the bread" (24:35).

The word and the bread! Disciples again and again experience Jesus as Lord in the Word of God and in the sacrament of broken bread.

When Jesus returned to show himself to the disciples, he invited them to touch his hands and feet (24:39). Some early Christians, influenced by Greek philosophical thought, began to teach that Jesus was a godlike spirit, once in human form, and that at death his spirit went to be with God. Luke, in reporting the Resurrection appearances, refuted this concept by showing the

66

transformed, resurrected Jesus eating a piece of broiled fish (24:42-43).

The Gospel of Luke, like Matthew and Mark, concludes with a Great Commission. In Luke, Jesus interpreted the Scriptures with a post-Resurrection perspective. "This is what is written: the Christ will suffer and rise from the dead on the third day, and a change of heart and life for the forgiveness of sins must be preached in his name to all nations, beginning from Jerusalem" (24:46-47). Jesus connected to Scripture the events that had happened. He was telling the apostles that they had seen Scripture fulfilled. And then he gave them the commission: "You are witnesses" (24:48). Just as Luke closed his Gospel with a blessing and with Jesus' being "taken up to heaven" (24:51), he opened Acts with the Ascension.

The Ascension is both the end and the beginning.

INTO THE WORLD

Witnessing with power and conviction is not easy. What attitudes, actions, or situations can get in the way of effective witness?

Some ways of witnessing are judgmental and "preachy" and put others down. What are some examples?

Witnessing requires an experience. What have you seen and heard in your spiritual journey about which you would gladly and honestly give witness?

Some people are gifted evangelists, able to witness in the homes of strangers. Call on one person this week, invite him or her to your church group or church. Listen a lot. Share something of your testimony.

DISCIPLE FAST TRACK

God's Word in My World

In what new ways will this session's message from God's Word influence my daily thoughts, attitudes, and actions so I continue to become more like Christ?

I will commit to integrating the above response into my daily living beginning this week by following this specific, measurable action:

IF YOU WANT TO KNOW MORE

All four Gospel writers present a Passion narrative, the arrest, trial, and crucifixion of Jesus: Matthew 26–27; Mark 14–15; Luke 22–23; John 18–19. Compare the accounts. Ask yourself what special emphasis Luke makes in his Passion account.

NOTES

"Repent, and be baptized every one of you in the name of Jesus Christ so that your sins may be forgiven; and you will receive the gift of the Holy Spirit. For the promise is for you, for your children, and for all who are far away, everyone whom the Lord our God calls to him." —Acts 2:38-39, NRSV

7 Acts of the Holy Spirit

OUR HUMAN CONDITION

When we think of power, we usually think about human resources. Position. Connections. An athlete may flex muscles. A businessperson may stress organization. A worker may point to the union. All of us know that money is power. Few of us turn to God for power. It seems like a strange request.

My commitment for "God's Word in My World" from our last session is:

ASSIGNMENT

Look at the last few verses of Luke and the first few verses of Acts to see the careful transition. Watch for common themes from Jesus' ministry as they recur in the witness of the apostles.

Savor the inexplicable power, the explosive force of the Holy Spirit. Notice carefully the results of Holy Spirit power.

SPIRITUAL DISCIPLINES

Guidance

God will guide us by the Holy Spirit, and through Spirit-filled persons and groups. We have only to be open and alert to that guidance.

When am I aware that the Holy Spirit is guiding me?

How will I practice this discipline this week?

Sabbath

Sabbath offers time for spiritual rest and renewal. We are instructed to wait and pray for the Holy Spirit. Are you in a hurry? Do you need spiritual renewal? Meditate on Isaiah 40:28-31. Pray for the indwelling Spirit of Christ in your heart.

Prayer

Pray daily before study:

> "LORD, let your faithful love surround us because we wait for you" (Psalm 33:22).

Prayer concerns for the week:

Day 1 **Read Acts 1** (Ascension, replacement for Judas).

Day 2 **Read Acts 2** (Pentecost, Peter's sermon, common fellowship).

Day 3 **Read Acts 3** (Peter and John heal a lame man).

Day 4 **Read Acts 4** (Peter and John before the Council, praying for boldness, shared possessions).

Day 5 **Read Acts 5** (Ananias and Sapphira, obey God not humans).

Day 6 **Read "Into the Word" and "Into the World" and answer the questions or provide responses.**

Day 7 **Rest, pray, and attend class.**

INTO THE WORD

Luke begins his second volume, also to Theophilus, with a handful of words recapping his Gospel. Then he mentioned that Jesus gave instructions to the apostles and "he showed them that he was alive with many convincing proofs" over a forty-day period (Acts 1:3). They were to wait in Jerusalem. Just as Luke's Gospel sets early events of Jesus' life in Jerusalem, so Luke's account of the beginnings of the church also is set in Jerusalem.

This chapter is titled "Acts of the Holy Spirit" because Luke's overriding interest was in showing the Spirit at work in and through the early church. Luke did not intend to write a comprehensive history of the early church. He gives us key events, mostly from the ministries of Peter and Paul, to help us understand the issues that confronted the early Christians.

Luke speaks immediately about the Holy Spirit, for just as the Holy Spirit entered Jesus at baptism and led him into the wilderness, so the Holy Spirit would lead the early church into the world.

"In only a few days you will be baptized with the Holy Spirit" (1:5). But the disciples asked a familiar question: "Lord, are you going to restore the kingdom to Israel now?" (1:6). They still couldn't get rid of their political Messiah notions. Jesus was patient. "It isn't for you to know the times. . . . Rather, you will receive power when the Holy Spirit has come upon you" (1:7-8).

The Ascension

Few teachings in the New Testament are treated so lightly by today's church as the ascension of Jesus. For Luke the experience is a crucial turning point. Jesus completed his ministry, walking the path of the suffering servant in perfect obedience. God raised him up in victory; and the transformed, resurrected Jesus appeared to the women, to Peter, to the two on the road to Emmaus, to five hundred, and to many others. His task on earth was finished. From the Mount of Olives, he ascended to the Father to be glorified. He took his full human experience into the experience of God. He ascended to be our great high priest (Hebrews 4:14). He departed so that he could come again in culmination of God's era of righteousness (Acts 1:11). But he also withdrew so that he could send the Holy Spirit upon the disciples. "They will do even greater works than these because I am going to the Father" (John 14:12).

"Why are you standing here, looking toward heaven?" (Acts 1:11). It was time to move on. God, who acted in Israel, who acted in Jesus Christ, was ready to act in and through the disciples. The Ascension marked the beginning of the empowerment of the church.

The disciples walked to the upper room in Jerusalem where other disciples were in prayer. The church would begin, even as Jesus' ministry began, on its knees.

Why did Peter insist that someone be chosen to take Judas's place? Because the symbolism of twelve was so important. Out of Israel the gospel had come. Now a new community of God's people would be going as witnesses, as light to the nations.

Peter spelled out the qualifications—one who had been with them from Jesus' baptism to the Ascension, one who would be a witness to the Resurrection (1:21-22). Two men were selected. Just as Jesus prayed before selecting the disciples, so they prayed. They cast lots (was this like the Urim and Thummim of the Hebrew high priest, Exodus 28:30?). They selected Matthias (Acts 1:26).

Pentecost

Pentecost was a Jewish festival. Originally an agricultural festival, it later became a celebration of the giving of the Law on Mount Sinai. Obedient to Jesus, all the believers were waiting and praying.

How do you describe a religious experience? What words can be used to explain a baptism of the Holy Spirit so strong, so vibrant, so complete that it changed the course of human history? Luke says it was like a fierce wind and that individual flames of fire appeared among them (2:2-4). They were filled with the Holy Spirit.

They began to speak in many different languages. Apparently they ran out into the streets, telling the story of faith. Jews from all over the world were gathered for the festival of Pentecost. They listened in amazement as these enthusiastic people spoke in the languages of the foreigners. Luke's message from Pentecost is that Christians, empowered by the Holy Spirit, will communicate the gospel in the languages of the people as Jesus had commanded, beginning "in Jerusalem, in all Judea and Samaria, and to the end of the earth" (1:8). Pentecost launched the missionary movement of the church.

Do you realize what God was doing? In the tower of Babel, people tried to do without God; so they were scattered. They could not communicate. Now at Pentecost people tried to listen to God, to empty themselves in obedience. God's Spirit swept them up into a perfect unity and enabled them to speak in every language of the world. Now in Christ people understood one another. We who were scattered are brought together in him. Pentecost was God's answer to Babel.

Notice that in Peter's sermon Luke provided us the core message of early Christian preaching. Observe his use of Hebrew Scripture as witness to Jesus. Study his explanation of the Crucifixion. Watch his reinterpretation of the Psalms. Look at the testimony to the Resurrection. Notice his reference to the Ascension and to the promise of the Holy Spirit.

But the sermon wasn't finished. As Jesus said, the purpose of preaching is to proclaim "a change of heart and life for the forgiveness of sins" (Luke 24:47). That day, three thousand were converted and were baptized (Acts 2:41). How are repentance and forgiveness of sins proclaimed in your church?

The Beautiful Gate

Luke and Acts used three expressions, all with the same meaning: "the Holy Spirit," "the Spirit of Jesus" (Acts 16:7), and "the Lord's Spirit" (Acts 5:9; 8:39). What is important for us to remember is that God is at work. The Holy Spirit does exactly the kinds of things Jesus did, for the Spirit is Jesus now with us. Christians across the centuries have struggled to understand the doctrine of the Trinity, but several key points are clear. We believe in one God. God has entered human history as Jesus. God's Spirit, the same Spirit that filled Jesus, is in the hearts and minds of believers.

So we are not surprised to discover Peter and John going to the Temple at the prescribed hour of prayer (Acts 3:1). Nor are we surprised as we read of their encounter with a man lame from birth, begging for alms (3:2). What would Jesus have done? Do you recall our Lord's parable of the great banquet (Luke 14:15-24)? Some guests refused to come, so the invitation was extended to "the poor, crippled, blind, and lame" (14:21). Do you remember the message Jesus sent to John the Baptist when John was in prison? *"Those who were blind are able to see. Those who were crippled now walk. People with skin diseases are cleansed. Those who were deaf now hear. Those who were dead are raised up. And good news is preached to the poor"* (7:22).

So we are not confused when Peter and John, empowered by the Spirit of Jesus, look intently at the man. Peter said, "I don't have any money, but I will give you what I do have. In the name of Jesus Christ the Nazarene, rise up and walk!" (Acts 3:6). Notice the reaction of the people to the healing of this man they had known so long as lame and asking alms. "They were filled with amazement and surprise" (3:10). Amazement and surprise are a common response in Luke's reporting. Watch for it.

Peter again used the moment for witnessing. Surely we ought to be more perceptive of interruptions that give us an opportunity to witness. Recall interruptions that allowed you to witness about your faith.

Look at Peter's sermon after the healing (3:11-26). First, he denied personal power or piety in the healing. Then he reminded them that the God of Abraham, Isaac, and Jacob is the God of Jesus. He referred to Jesus, crucified under Pilate, "the very one whom God raised from the dead. We are witnesses of this" (3:15). The lame man was healed "because of faith in Jesus' name" (3:16). But there is more. Peter offered repentance to the listeners right then and there "so that your sins may be wiped away" (3:19).

The refrain of repentance and forgiveness is a favorite of Luke's. Other New Testament writers tell of redemption, reconciliation, regeneration, and rebirth. Each image has power: Redemption pictures a slave being bought and freed. Reconciliation shows two people embracing, a restoration of a relationship. But debts are forgiven. The term is a business term. The New Testament writers were not finicky about where they got words. Sin is not merely making mistakes. We are born with a mortgage on our hands. As part of the family of humankind, we have a fantastic pile of back payments. We are in debt to the God of holiness. But Jesus is the judge. We cannot repay the debt, for it is overwhelming. Only Jesus Christ can forgive it, cancel it, wipe it away. The good news is that for the one who repents, who trusts, the debt is canceled. In the Lord's Prayer, Jesus taught us to pray, "Forgive us for the ways we have wronged you [forgive us our debts]" (Matthew 6:12, CEB, NRSV), "Forgive us our sins" (Luke 11:4, CEB). Have you experienced the freedom of having your debts canceled?

The Council

By the time Luke wrote Acts, Christians had been persecuted in different places for various reasons. Stephen, a Hellenistic Jew, had been martyred in Jerusalem at the hands of Jewish authorities. New churches around the eastern Mediterranean experienced rejection, sometimes with physical violence. Gentiles were angry when worship in their temples and the sale of idols were undermined. Some Jewish leaders who had doctrinal differences with Christians opposed them with force.

Some Roman emperors caused havoc. Caligula tried to erect a statue of himself in the Temple in Jerusalem. He drove Jews from Rome as undesirables. Nero, in A.D. 64, in a fit of madness and rage, slaughtered Christians, probably including Paul and Peter.

So when Luke wrote about Peter and John being arrested and taken before the Council in Jerusalem, he had two motives. First, he intended to put steel in the backbones of believers who were suffering for their faith. Just as his Gospel recorded Jesus' warning of persecutions to come, so Acts reports resistance to the Christian movement from the very beginning.

Also, Luke wanted Roman civil authorities, as well as Jewish authorities, to understand that Christians were not insurrectionists, not violent revolutionaries. The persecutions were not only futile but needless as well.

Peter and John were arrested by the Temple guard and later taken before the Council. The Romans, during the years of occupation, appointed the high priest to guarantee cooperation. Some respected

Pharisees were on the Council. So were some Sadducees, representing powerful families who worked with the Roman authorities to try to keep Temple worship alive, maintain order, and avoid confrontation so that business life could go on.

Already Christian Jews numbered five thousand, so the Jewish leaders were concerned. Their fear was both political (the people called Jesus Messiah) and religious (that Temple worship was under attack).

Peter boldly asked if they were on trial because "something good was done for a sick person" (Acts 4:9). Then he used the opportunity to witness to the crucifixion and resurrection of Jesus. He quoted the psalm that Jesus had quoted about "the stone rejected by the builders" (Psalm 118:22), but Peter made it personal: "the stone *you* builders rejected" (Acts 4:11, emphasis added). The boldness to say "Salvation can be found in no one else" (4:12) was an affront to the Jewish leaders on their home turf. Because of the dramatic healing, right on the steps of the Temple, the authorities were afraid to act harshly, so they ordered Peter and John to cease preaching. Christians across the centuries have been fortified by Peter and John's response: "It's up to you to determine whether it's right before God to obey you rather than God. As for us, we can't stop speaking about what we have seen and heard" (4:19-20).

After the disciples' release, the church moved into a time of prayer. What did they pray for? For confidence! That prayer was powerfully answered (4:31; 5:12-16).

After more "signs and wonders," healings and conversions, the high priest took action (5:17-18). Peter and other apostles not named were arrested and put in the public prison. After a wondrous escape, they preached again at daybreak and again were apprehended. In their defense, Peter reaffirmed that "the God of our ancestors raised Jesus" (5:30). Luke wanted us to know that sometimes the authorities are afraid; sometimes they are not. On occasion the jail doors are opened (12:1-19), but at other times they remain locked. Confident witness can bring amazement. It can also result in martyrdom. But the witness remained confident, bold, and courageous.

Luke introduced a brave personality during the apostles' trial (5:33-34). His name was Gamaliel, a Pharisee, a respected teacher and member of the Council. At first his advice seemed merely prudent, but then he valiantly suggested God might be in the movement. So God used a Pharisee to save the apostles. Help can come from many places. The apostles were flogged and let go, "rejoicing because they had been regarded as worthy to suffer disgrace for the sake of the name" (5:41).

Hints of the Jerusalem Church

Luke wanted us to know that Greek-speaking Jews were already in the church. Look at Barnabas and at Ananias and Sapphira. Barnabas's real name was Joseph, but the apostles affectionately renamed him Barnabas, meaning "one who encourages" (4:36). He had been a Jew of the Diaspora, one of five million Jews living outside of Palestine. He was born on the island of Cyprus, a Levite, a cousin of John Mark (Colossians 4:10), but was now living in Jerusalem. Thousands of Hellenized Jews lived in Jerusalem. They spoke Greek; wore Greek or Mediterranean style clothes; went to athletic contests; used the Septuagint, the Greek translation of the Scripture; shaved their beards; and sometimes were lax about keeping the law of Moses.

In his early spiritual enthusiasm, Barnabas sold his property, took all the money and "placed it in the care and under the authority of the apostles" (Acts 4:37). The apostles quickly identified his depth of commitment. Luke wrote of Barnabas, "He was a good man, whom the Holy Spirit had endowed with exceptional faith" (11:24). Barnabas helped Paul begin his ministry. He made arduous missionary journeys, and he was sent by conservatives and liberals as an emissary, one to the other. Barnabas was so honest and so kind that he had everyone's respect.

Perhaps in contrast to Barnabas, Luke introduced Ananias and Sapphira, husband and wife. They sold their property, hid part of the money, brought the rest, and laid it at the apostles' feet (5:1-2). The story is not a stewardship sermon. Money was not the issue; the issue was truth and community. Peter made it clear. No one asked them to sell their property. They were not obligated to give the money to the church. But Peter understood that the church had power because it was honest. Miracles happened because love abounded. People were vulnerable, laid bare to one another, confessing their sins to one another, praying for one another. No wonder healings of all sorts took place.

Now came a couple smuggling a lie into the fellowship. Their deception mocked the Holy Spirit. Peter knew the deception was a life-or-death matter for the church, as indeed it was also for Ananias and Sapphira.

Any pretense in the life of Christ's fellowship threatens the openness, trust, unity, and love essential for the Holy Spirit to work among us.

INTO THE WORLD

Sometimes we witness by our integrity, our actions, our ministries. Sometimes we talk favorably about our church, our study group, or our pastor. But when and how might we talk about our faith? Where can we testify to the living Lord? To whom can we speak of such intimate matters as forgiveness, assurance, healing of soul or body, strength of Christian fellowship and prayer?

DISCIPLE FAST TRACK

Pray for the Holy Spirit to show you a person to whom you might speak. Pray for power to witness effectively. You may need to listen for a while before you speak. Pray for wisdom and for courage.

God's Word in My World

In what new ways will this session's message from God's Word influence my daily thoughts, attitudes, and actions so I continue to become more like Christ?

I will commit to integrating the above response into my daily living beginning this week by following this specific, measurable action:

IF YOU WANT TO KNOW MORE

The *Hellenists* in Acts were Greek-speaking Jewish Christians influenced by Greek customs and culture. Many of them were from Jewish families that had been living outside Palestine for several generations, so they had lost touch with much of their Jewish heritage and their sense of separateness. For them the synagogue was the center of worship.

The *Hebrews* in Acts were Aramaic-speaking Jewish Christians, probably mostly natives of Palestine, who were much less influenced by Greek culture. For them the Temple was the center of worship, and the requirements of the law of Moses insured their separateness as the people of God.

The *God-fearers* were not Jews. They were Gentiles who attended synagogue and Temple services as guests and kept some of the requirements of the law of Moses and some of the Jewish food laws without undergoing circumcision to become full converts to Judaism.

"As they were worshipping the Lord and fasting, the Holy Spirit said, 'Appoint Barnabas and Saul to the work I have called them to undertake.' After they fasted and prayed, they laid their hands on these two and sent them off."

—Acts 13:2-3

8 The Gospel Begins to Spread

OUR HUMAN CONDITION

Some people insist their way of believing is better than some other way. Everyone has his or her own beliefs. Even if I do share my beliefs, I'm not sure I have the power, strength, or convictions to really convince anybody to believe differently anyway.

My commitment for "God's Word in My World" from our last session is:

ASSIGNMENT

The gospel witness spreads—first to Judean Jews; then Hellenistic Jews; then Samaritans; then God-fearers, foreigners, and Gentiles. Watch it spread, fueled by the blood of Stephen.

The conversion of Saul prepares the way for his mighty missionary work and his powerful writings. The big issue was the continual need for interpreting to Jewish Christians the conversion and Holy Spirit experience of Gentiles. It was a major miracle that the church held together.

SPIRITUAL DISCIPLINES

Fasting
In the act of fasting, we refocus attention in order to make a decision, seek direction, or experience freedom.

How will I practice this discipline this week?

Sabbath
The Antioch church was fasting when the Holy Spirit convicted them to send missionaries. A fast can be any form of abstinence—from food, from television or radio. On this Sabbath consider eating a light meal and spending some time quietly.

Prayer
Pray daily before study:

> "My Lord! There is no one like you
>   among the gods!
> There is nothing that can compare
>   to your works!
> All the nations that you've made will come
>   and bow down before you, Lord;
>   they will glorify your name,
>   because you are awesome
>   and a wonder-worker.
>   You are God. Just you" (Psalm 86:8-10).

Prayer concerns for the week:

Day 1 **Read Acts 6** (seven deacons, Stephen charged); **Acts 7** (Stephen's speech, first martyr); **Acts 8** (Philip, Peter, and John in Samaria; the Ethiopian).

Day 2 **Read Acts 9:1-31** (Saul's conversion); **Galatians 1** (Paul an apostle).

Day 3 **Read Acts 9:32–10:48** (healing of Aeneas and Dorcas; Peter and Cornelius); **Acts 11** (Peter reports about Gentiles, called Christians in Antioch).

Day 4 **Read Acts 12** (James martyred, Peter freed); **Acts 13–14** (Barnabas and Saul sent as missionaries).

Day 5 **Read Acts 15:1-35** (Jerusalem Council); **Galatians 2** (Paul, an apostle).

Day 6 Read **"Into the Word" and "Into the World" and answer the questions or provide responses.**

Day 7 Rest, pray, and attend class.

INTO THE WORD

Jerusalem bubbled like a boiling pot. Ever since Herod the Great died shortly after the birth of Jesus, all semblance of Jewish independence disappeared. Rome ruled directly and ruled tough. The great census taken by Augustus Caesar was a massive tax plan. Jews resented tribute money being extracted from them to be sent to Rome. Friction was never-ending. When Judea got behind in paying tribute, the Roman procurator made up the deficit by raiding the Temple bank.

After the crucifixion of Jesus, political and social life deteriorated further. From the Roman standpoint, the Jews' strange ways and independent spirit were sources of constant irritation. Some freedom fighter, an insurrectionist, a self-styled "Messiah," was constantly rising up. Roman soldiers would quash each rebellion.

The Roman procurators ruled from Caesarea, the artificial Mediterranean harbor built by Herod the Great to honor Caesar Augustus. A steady stream of Roman soldiers embarked and disembarked from Caesarea. They controlled Jerusalem not only with soldiers but by appointing the high priest who was supposed to serve for life.

Jewish followers of Jesus, as yet without a name, were simply a "Nazarene" sect holding one messianic opinion in a swirl of opinions. Even though the followers were all of one mind immediately after Pentecost, gradually they too had differing viewpoints.

For example, differences erupted between the Judean Jews and the Hellenistic Jews. We saw first signs with the complaint of the widows. But deeper issues, theological and moral conflicts surfaced. Judean Jews like the apostles, the early converts, and Mary the mother of Jesus intensified their prayer life, obeyed the law of Moses as Jesus had radically interpreted it, went regularly to the Temple, and broke bread in one another's homes. James the brother of Jesus did not become a convert until after he experienced Jesus in resurrection. Then he slowly became a leader of the Jerusalem church, particularly the Hebrew core.

On the other hand, Hellenist Jewish converts, like Stephen, were less compelled by laws and rituals. The Greek-speaking Jewish converts seemed to be more evangelistic. When they were scattered by persecution, they witnessed and created communities of faith wherever they went.

How did Christians feel about the political situation? Neither Hellenists nor Hebrews were Zealots. Even though Jesus was crucified between two insurrectionists with the slogan "King of the Jews" nailed above his head, his followers knew that he had not come to rally an army. Jesus turned his back on political revolution. His advice on taxes was middle ground, implying that, since Caesar's image was on the coins, they should hand them back to him.

What about the Temple, symbol of Jewish nationalism? Different thoughts circulated. Some thought that end times were at hand. The storm clouds of political tension underlined thoughts of calamity. Many believed that if the Temple were destroyed, it would be God's judgment, as surely as in the days of the Assyrians and the Babylonians. They also remembered that Jesus had said they should flee when the city began to be destroyed. Already many people were doing just that.

So in this period between A.D. 30 and the Jewish rebellion of A.D. 66, we see the Jerusalem church becoming more conservative, more Jewish, struggling to survive in the stronghold of Judaism. We observe Hellenistic Jews scattering as refugees always must do, to relatives, friends, or anywhere they could make a living and survive. After the destruction of Jerusalem in A.D. 70, even most of the Hebrew believers were scattered or killed.

Stephen's Speech

Stephen wisely reaffirmed his position as a Jew, starting with respectful "Brothers and fathers," then recalling Hebrew history beginning with Abraham. All went well until Stephen began to hint of complaints against Moses (Acts 7:35).

Looking the Council members in the eye, Stephen tied them to an apostate Israel, linking them with the Israel the prophets condemned. It is one thing to speak historically, to recall the sins of people way back when. It is another thing to say, "You stubborn people! In your thoughts and hearing, you are like those who have had no part in God's covenant! You continuously set yourself against the Holy Spirit, just like your ancestors did" (Acts 7:51). Stephen seemed to be recalling Jesus, who referred to the death of the prophets: "How terrible for you! You built memorials to the prophets, whom your ancestors killed. . . . God's wisdom has said, 'I will send prophets and apostles to them and they will harass and kill some of them.' As a result, this generation will be charged with the murder of all the prophets since the beginning of time" (Luke 11:47-50).

Stephen's conclusion was his witness (remember the Greek word for witness is *martyr*). They, the Israelites of old, killed those who foretold the coming of Jesus, and now "you've betrayed and murdered him" (Acts 7:52). Then, as a final indictment, "You received the Law given by angels, but you haven't kept it" (7:53).

Stephen's Offense

How did Stephen offend them? First, he focused on Israel's sins. In the eyes of the contemporary religious authorities, they were holding the faith against Gentiles and heathens, especially against heretics. They saw themselves as bastions of faithfulness. Second, at a time when at any moment the Roman legions could demolish the Temple as King Nebuchadnezzar had done, they were selling their souls to defend it against all threats. Now came a Greek-speaking Jew reminding *them* that God has heaven for a throne and earth for a footstool (7:49). Stephen was clearly a follower of the One who made mysterious threats about destroying the Temple and rebuilding it in three days (John 2:19). Third, he blamed them for killing God's Messiah as their fathers had killed the prophets. Fourth, he accused them of not keeping the Law.

Three observations. First, some courageous men buried Stephen at the risk of their lives. Second, the witnesses who threw stones at Stephen placed their outer garments at the feet of a young Pharisee named Saul. "Saul was in full agreement with Stephen's murder" (8:1). Third, a persecution, directed at all Christian Jews but especially at Hellenistic Christian Jews, began sweeping through the streets of the city. Saul and others went from house to house, dragging the believers from their homes and throwing them into prison.

Philip's Mission

Luke introduced Philip the evangelist to us in Acts 6:5 when the seven deacons were chosen to look after the widows. He should not be confused with Philip the apostle (Luke 6:14; John 1:43-46).

Luke carefully used Philip the evangelist to make a point. The persecution will be used by God for good. The believers scattered into the countryside of Judea and Samaria, where they immediately "moved on, preaching the good news along the way" (Acts 8:4).

But Luke had more in mind. The first believers were Judean Jews. Next came Hellenized Jews, like Stephen and Philip. Then the word went to Samaria, even as Jesus had commanded. In a world where ethnic and religious identity was so important, one boundary after another was being crossed.

What boundaries have you and your church been able to cross with the gospel?

Saul's Conversion

Saul, Roman citizen of Tarsus, full Jew of the tribe of Benjamin, Pharisee according to the Law, student of the leading rabbi Gamaliel, committed himself to stamp out heresy. He not only approved when Stephen was stoned, not only helped drag Jews who believed in Jesus out of their homes, but he went even further. He volunteered to go to other towns and chase down Christians. Already believers were known to be in towns and cities throughout the area. How fast the community was expanding!

Saul took letters of introduction from the high priest to the synagogues in Damascus, intending to bring any Christians back to Jerusalem (Acts 9:1-2).

For Paul, the important point about his conversion was that the word came from Jesus himself: "It came through a revelation from Jesus Christ" (Galatians 1:12). Others might be converted

NOTES

by preaching, by healing, by witnessing. Saul was called, personally and directly, by Jesus. Saul now became a witness.

Apostle to the Gentiles

When Saul traveled to Jerusalem, three years had passed since his conversion and call (Galatians 1:18). All through his ministry Paul was defensive when some said he was not a true apostle, or especially if they argued that they were superior. To the Galatians he insisted that God had set him apart, like Jeremiah, before he was born. He was called by God's grace as surely as the fishermen beside the Sea of Galilee. Saul had seen the risen, living Christ as surely as had the disciples (1 Corinthians 15:8). He too knew the power of the Holy Spirit, for he had been swept up to heaven (2 Corinthians 12:2), an experience of the Holy Spirit not unlike that of the one hundred twenty at Pentecost (Acts1:15).

So when Saul went to Jerusalem to visit with Peter, he did not go to receive the gospel; he went for fellowship and to confer. When he spoke with James, the Lord's brother, he did not do it to receive Christ's Spirit but to talk, believer to believer.

If there are watersheds in Christian history, Peter's visit to Cornelius is one of them. Philip already had journeyed to Caesarea; perhaps he laid the groundwork (Acts 8:40). Cornelius, a career Roman soldier, had become a man of great faith (10:2). A Gentile, he was a God-fearer, praying, reading the Scripture, giving alms. While he was in prayer, an angel told him about Peter—imagine this— lodging with a tanner in Joppa. Cornelius immediately sent a trusted soldier and two slaves to invite Peter to Caesarea (10:7-8).

As the envoys journeyed south along the coast toward Joppa the next day, Peter went up on Simon the tanner's roof to pray. He fell into a spiritual trance. In his vision, a sheet full of animals, reptiles, and birds descended from heaven, lowered by its four corners. "Heaven" meant from God; "four corners" reflected the whole earth; the living creatures included both clean and unclean.

It is hard for us to remember why certain foods were declared unclean by the law of Moses. But the Scriptures are absolutely clear: The food laws were meant to separate God's covenant people from all others. The Jews were to be different, a chosen people set apart, living by carefully prescribed laws.

Not to circumcise, not to eat proper foods, or not to observe Sabbath was not to be a Jew! But God said to Peter three times, "Never consider unclean what God has made pure" (10:15).

The three men appeared, as if from God. Peter invited them in, two Gentile slaves and a Roman soldier, and gave them lodging (10:23). He gave hospitality.

The next day they traveled to Caesarea. At Cornelius's house Peter proclaimed, "I really am learning that God doesn't show partiality to one group of people over another" (10:34). He then told the story of Jesus' ministry, his cross, and his resurrection. Peter testified to his experiences with the risen Christ and said that everyone who believed in Christ would receive forgiveness of sins.

DISCIPLE FAST TRACK

NOTES

While Peter was speaking, the Holy Spirit came upon the group. Jewish believers who had come with Peter were amazed. He ordered Cornelius and his household to be baptized. Peter and his fellow Jewish believers stayed with Cornelius, participating in table fellowship for several days.

Consider the drastic change in attitude and practice required by Peter's vision. What situation can you imagine that would cause you to make as drastic a change in attitude and practice?

Back in Jerusalem, Peter was called on the carpet by the conservative Jewish believers for eating with Cornelius (11:1-3). Gradually now Luke begins to call them "the circumcised" party. More than a thousand years of tradition about food laws stood under scrutiny. Remember, James the brother of Jesus was listening as well as the other apostles. When Peter finished, "they praised God and concluded, 'So then God has enabled Gentiles to change their hearts and lives so that they might have new life'" (11:18). Instead of remaining a Jewish sect, Christianity was destined to break out of Judaism and spread to the whole world.

Some believers fled to Antioch from the Jerusalem persecution (11:19). Others came from Cyprus and as far away as Cyrene in today's Libya (11:20). As these believers prayed and witnessed, still others were converted, people from all walks of life—Aramaic-speaking Jews, Greek-speaking Jews, God-fearing Gentiles, and for the first time ordinary run-of-the-mill Gentiles.

First Missionaries

The Antioch church was in spiritual ferment (Acts 13:1). Christian leaders from all over the world gravitated there. Barnabas's cousin John Mark was there. Saul was there. So was Simeon (nicknamed Niger), and a Cyrenean named Lucius. A member of Herod's court, a man named Manaen, was there. Several of the apostles, including Peter, visited and preached.

Fasting was a key ingredient in their worship. As the Antioch church was fasting and in prayer, the Holy Spirit moved upon them. Luke is very clear that the same Spirit that led Jesus into ministry and exploded on Pentecost now initiated the formal missionary movement. "The Holy Spirit said, 'Appoint Barnabas and Saul to the work I have called them to undertake'" (13:2).

So the church fasted, prayed, and laid hands on Barnabas and Saul and "sent them off" (13:3). To where? In your study Bible or online, look carefully at a map of Paul's first missionary journey. Notice the eastern and western part of Cyprus, the harbor on the southern coast (modern-day Turkey). Then look for the interior towns of Antioch, Iconium, Lystra, and Derbe. By water and land, the trip covered over a thousand miles.

Notice the pattern that continued in subsequent missionary trips. They went first to the synagogue, where they witnessed. They stayed in homes of those who were sympathetic. Their message created confusion and division, but some people were converted among both Jews and God-fearing Gentiles. Repercussions and recriminations came from the resistant Jewish community, sometimes as strong as a frightful stoning that almost killed Paul (14:19). The anger was so great that some of the Jews followed them from one city to another. So Paul began to say, "We will turn to the Gentiles," using Isaiah 49:6 as scriptural authority (Acts 13:46-48).

Jerusalem Council

Some of the conservative Judean Jews who were believers traveled to Antioch and were aghast that new Gentile Christians were not being circumcised (Acts 15:1-2). In their experience, a person could become a proselyte Jewish Christian but couldn't be saved unless circumcised (15:1). Paul and Barnabas took issue for two reasons. First, they had observed repentance and forgiveness, the signs of true conversion, among Gentiles who had not been circumcised, and the experience of the Holy Spirit, the sign of the real baptism of Jesus. Therefore, circumcision was not a prior condition for salvation or now a required result. Second, Paul especially understood that if a convert took on the law of Moses, that person took on everything. Circumcision meant more than ritual; it bound one to all the requirements of the Law.

It is a tribute to the Holy Spirit and to the church that no split occurred. Antioch sent a delegation to Jerusalem, for the apostles still carried the authority. Both sides were heard thoroughly. Then Peter again told about his vision and the outpouring of the Holy Spirit on Cornelius.

How have you seen the outpouring of the Holy Spirit at work in you?

James the brother of Jesus, leader of the Law-observing, conservative Hebrew element, offered a compromise: No circumcision would be required (that satisfied Paul and Barnabas). But several requirements so sensitive that any Jew would be revolted if they were violated were retained: No eating of food that had been placed on heathen altars and then sold in the meat shops. No drinking of blood or eating animals from which blood had not been drained. No sexual promiscuity and fornication (15:19-20). All agreed. The congregation in Antioch rejoiced. Unity in the church was preserved. The door for the gospel was wide open to Jews and Gentiles all over the world.

How have you seen the door for the gospel opened?

INTO THE WORLD

Our world, like the ancient world, is made up of many language, racial, and cultural groups, making communication difficult. Yet the Holy Spirit drives believers across those lines in missionary activity.

Many of our churches are culturally comfortable. So many of us don't know how to go out into the world. It is easier to give money, support missions programs, or have supper with friends.

How can I actually learn to go myself? How can our DISCIPLE FAST TRACK group choose and cross some barrier together? Who? When? What ideas can I bring to my group?

What barrier will I cross on my own? When? How?

God's Word in My World

In what new ways will this session's message from God's Word influence my daily thoughts, attitudes, and actions so I continue to become more like Christ?

I will commit to integrating the above response into my daily living beginning this week by following this specific, measurable action:

IF YOU WANT TO KNOW MORE

So many Bible maps give names of cities, regions, and countries that either have ceased to exist or now have other names. Find a modern map and trace the various missionary journeys; locate the different regions, countries, cities, islands, and rivers in their current geographical context. Keep them in mind as you follow world events reported in daily news.

NOTES

"He [the jailer] brought them into his home and gave them a meal. He was overjoyed because he and everyone in his household had come to believe in God."　　—Acts 16:34

9　Rejoice in the Lord

OUR HUMAN CONDITION

I am happy when things go well, sad when they don't. I guess if I had enough money or friends, people would treat me right and I would be happy all the time. People tell me how I should live, but none of it makes sense as far as being happy is concerned.

My commitment for "God's Word in My World" from our last session is:

ASSIGNMENT

Part of the fun of this lesson is in putting together what we know about Philippi from history, from Acts, and from Paul's letter. God sends a clear vision, so Paul races to Philippi. Look at different missionary approaches: in Lydia's home in Philippi, in the synagogue in Thessalonica, and on Mars Hill in Athens.

SPIRITUAL DISCIPLINES

Celebration
When we move from a self-centered existence to a God-centered existence, we move from anxiety to joy.

How will I practice this discipline this week?

Sabbath
Sabbath shapes our attitudes and activities in the coming week. On this Sabbath allow yourself simply to *be* rather than to *do*. Let Sabbath renew you, changing you and changing the days ahead.

Prayer
Pray daily before study:

"It is good to give thanks to the LORD,
　　to sing praises to your name,
　　　　Most High;
to proclaim your loyal love in the
　　　　morning,
　　your faithfulness at nighttime"
　　　　　　　(Psalm 92:1-2).

Prayer concerns for the week:

Day 1 **Read Acts 15:36–16:15** (Paul's second missionary journey, vision of Macedonia).

Day 2 **Read Acts 16:16-40** (Paul heals possessed girl, the Philippian jailer).

Day 3 **Read Acts 17** (uproar in Thessalonica, courtesy in Athens).

Day 4 **Read Philippians 1–2** (Paul rejoices in prison, Christ's humility).

Day 5 **Read Philippians 3–4** (warning, Paul's gain in Christ, rejoice).

Day 6 **Read "Into the Word" and "Into the World" and answer the questions or provide responses.**

Day 7 **Rest, pray, and attend class.**

DISCIPLE FAST TRACK

INTO THE WORD

NOTES

Paul was a man of truth; Barnabas was a man of love. Paul knew that John Mark got homesick and deserted them on their first missionary journey (in Pamphylia, Acts 15:37-38). Barnabas knew the lad was his cousin (Colossians 4:10) and a friend of Peter.

When Christians differ, they sometimes shake hands and separate. That's what Barnabas and Paul did, and God used their conflict to fuel the missionary cause. Barnabas took young John Mark and set sail for Cyprus. Paul took Silas, who had helped carry the letter of conciliation from the Council in Jerusalem, and they walked overland into Asia Minor (Acts 15:37-41).

Paul knew the territory, now modern Turkey. He was raised in Tarsus, a large seaport city, and his first missionary trip had taken him to the interior towns, Derbe, Lystra, and Iconium. As they traveled, they encouraged the churches, won new converts, and carried news from Jerusalem and Syrian Antioch, including word of the great compromise.

At Lystra they found a serious young Christian named Timothy, perhaps an earlier convert of Paul's (16:1). His father was Greek; his mother, Jewish. Paul asked Timothy to join them, which began a relationship so deep it was like father and son.

Years later, in his letter to Rome, Paul called him "my coworker" (Romans 16:21). In his final days in prison, what joy it gave Paul to have Timothy visit him. "I have no one like him. . . . He labors with me for the gospel like a son works with his father" (Philippians 2:20-22).

Why did Paul have Timothy circumcised (Acts 16:3)? Even though Paul had won permission for Greeks to become converts without it, Timothy was a special case. His mother was Jewish; even today that is a primary definition for being a Jew. Both Jews and Jewish Christians would be offended for Paul to travel with an uncircumcised Jew. Look at 1 Corinthians 9:19-23. What did Paul mean when he said he tried to become "all things to all people" (9:22)?

Now a strange thing occurred. Paul's plans were to continue into Asia. But the Holy Spirit intervened (Acts 16:6). Again his itinerary pointed toward the Black Sea, "but the Spirit of Jesus wouldn't let them" go (16:7). Instead, at the seaport of Troas, near historic Troy (site of the Trojan War), Paul had a powerful vision during the night. A man appeared, pleading with him and saying, "Come over to Macedonia and help us!" (16:9).

Paul, Silas, and Timothy set sail. But wait. The language changes in Acts 16:10. Suddenly the word is *we;* the author, Luke, seems to have joined the group. Where did this Gentile Christian

92

doctor come from? We do not know, but he wrote as a participant in Acts 16:10-17; 20:5-15; 21:1-18; 27:1–28:16.

The group sailed, pulled by the knowledge that they were going where God wanted them to go. One day's sail put them on the island of Samothrace. A second day brought them to Neapolis. The seaport for Philippi was ten miles away.

When have you faced watershed times with irrevocable decisions to go one way or another that shaped your destiny?

A Roman Colony

Philippi was a Roman colony, established by Marc Antony late in the first century B.C. The mixture of people in Philippi meant a mixture of religions. Roman gods, Greek gods, Stoic philosophers, some Egyptian influences, probably a few mystery societies—Philippi had them all. For the first time, the gospel pointed toward pure Gentile territory. Paul was ready to begin his first church in Europe.

Always before Paul had started at the synagogue, but Philippi had no synagogue. Only a handful of Jews and a few women God-fearers joined on the Sabbath outside the city on the banks of the river for prayer. So that is where Paul, Timothy, Silas, and Luke began (Acts 16:13).

A remarkable woman named Lydia listened intently. She came from Thyatira near Pergamum in Asia Minor, noted for its dyeing works. She was an independent businesswoman, trading in luxurious purple cloth and garments (16:14). Purple, the king's color, was expensive because it came from mollusks, shellfish in the waters of Syria and Phoenicia.

Lydia asked to be baptized; and she included her entire household—servants, perhaps children, and even slaves. Then she urged the itinerant preachers to receive hospitality in her home. We do not hear of Lydia again in the New Testament. Paul does not mention her in greetings to his beloved Philippian church. Her hometown later contained a strong Christian church, as we discover in Revelation where John wrote to the seven churches (Revelation 2:18-29).

A Song in the Night

Usually the missionaries met theological conflict in the synagogue. In Philippi the problem was economic. When Paul healed the young psychic, he stripped her owners of their livelihood (Acts 16:16-19).

Roman law prevailed in Philippi, but the two slaveowners had friends. They dragged Paul and Silas before some magistrates and in a mob moment, had them stripped, beaten, and thrown into jail (16:20-23). The jailer, probably a conscientious Roman soldier, on duty, "threw them into the innermost cell and secured their feet in stocks" (16:24).

Few images are more inspiring than Paul and Silas, backs bleeding, feet in chains, singing hymns and psalms at midnight as the other prisoners listened (16:25). One of the psalms declares, "by night his song is with me" (Psalm 42:8). What a spiritual victory to be able to praise God and sing in life's midnight hours!

The area around Philippi is known for its earthquakes. This quake was powerful and providential (Acts 16:26). A Roman soldier might be executed for being derelict in his duty. With his jail in shambles, thinking the prisoners gone, he drew his sword to commit suicide rather than suffer shame (16:27). Paul stopped him. Then the man and his whole household were baptized in the name of the Lord Jesus. The Gentile jailer washed their Jewish wounds, put food before them (the jailer is eating with the prisoners), and "was overjoyed because he and everyone in his household had come to believe in God" (16:34).

With dignity Paul and the others walked to Lydia's home, encouraged the new believers, and then departed (16:40).

A Sophisticated City

Moving southwest, the missionaries did a powerful work in Thessalonica. "As was Paul's custom," he and his associates went to the synagogue (Acts 17:2). Once again some Jews were converted as well as "a larger number of Greek God-worshippers and quite a few prominent women" (17:4). The newly formed church sent the missionaries on to Beroea where they obtained a good reception in the synagogue and received a few "reputable Greek women and many Greek men" (17:10-12). When trouble came, Timothy and Silas remained; Luke is not mentioned. Paul hurried on alone, taking a sailboat to the capital city.

Paul, like every tourist, hit Athens with stars in his eyes. Tarsus, his home city, was a strong cultural and educational center; but Athens had no peer. Even Rome, military and political capital of the empire, deferred to Athens in scholarship, philosophy, fine arts, and culture.

Paul reasoned in the synagogue and talked with people in the *agora,* the marketplace where all the news and gossip circulated (17:17). Statues of Greek and Roman gods were everywhere: Zeus, Nike, Venus, Neptune, and many more. Of course, dominating the city of a quarter million people was the Acropolis, literally "top of the city," the tower hill thrusting the Parthenon into the blue Mediterranean sky. Today's tourists see majestic ruins of this twenty-four-hundred-year-old temple to Athena, but Paul saw it glistening in all its architectural wonder.

Athens, city of Socrates, Plato, and Aristotle, was proud not only of its centuries of philosophic debate but also of its tradition of democracy. However, that democracy was limited to citizens— the high-born, the educated, the property holders. Most of the population were slaves.

NOTES

Among the educated people swirled a constant stream of religious and philosophic thought. The Epicureans taught that the individual should seek happiness by doing whatever brings contentment. Both body and soul were important, but death ended all.

The Stoics believed that the universe was orderly, not capricious, that reason was supreme, and that fate governed a person's life. The universe was cyclical and timeless. The soul may be immortal. If we live in harmony with the laws of nature, we will have inner peace and well-being. But Stoicism was cold, rational, with no relationship to a personal God, no opportunity for forgiveness.

The mystery cults were less intellectual, more emotional. The goal was immortality. The method was to join a mystery religion and be carefully prepared—perhaps by fasting, sexual abstinence, living for a night or a week in a darkened cave—to be initiated into the life of the gods. The goal was to *experience* a moment with the gods, to be a secret initiate into special knowledge.

Scarcely a religion, but a powerful set of ideas floated around that would plague Christianity for centuries, even today. Called Gnosticism, from *gnosis,* meaning knowledge or wisdom, it sprang from the Greek ideas that spirit is good and matter, especially the body, is evil. The created physical order, at best, is a passing shadow of reality that imprisons us in corruption. One's only salvation lies in escape, a spiritual release for those who acquire spiritual knowledge.

We quickly see the conflict of these ideas with Genesis, when God saw everything that was created and "it was supremely good" (Genesis 1:31). Gnosticism also conflicts with the Incarnation in the New Testament. The church insists that Jesus experienced full humanity. The Apostles' Creed was written to refute Gnosticism by saying Jesus was born, suffered, was crucified, dead, and buried, and to affirm Jesus' completely human experience. Jesus was not just a spirit in a shell of earthly experience.

So when Paul walked up that hill in Athens called the Areopagus, the site of the oldest law court in the world, he must have been excited. Scholars and philosophers gathered to hear new ideas. They had heard him babble in the marketplace; now they invited him to speak.

Read Paul's speech in Acts 17:22-31. He once told the Corinthian church that he did not come to them as an "expert in speech or wisdom" (1 Corinthians 2:1). Here, with the scholars, Paul became the perfect diplomat. Speaking in sophisticated Greek, carefully flattering their interest in religion, he pointed to the altar to the unknown god (Acts 17:23). That altar was an attempt to touch every base. Then Paul related some Jewish history, which they understood, for they had read the Septuagint. Some prominent Jews lived in the city. He quoted Greek poets, affirmed Stoics and Epicureans in denying capricious gods. He underlined the greatness of God.

But when Paul testified to the resurrection of Jesus, they shook their heads (17:31-32). Some sneered. They could have handled immortality of the soul, but not a resurrection of the body from the dead. No wonder Paul later wrote that the cross is "a scandal to Jews" (how could Messiah be crucified?) and "foolishness to Gentiles" (how could a man be raised from the dead?) (1 Corinthians 1:23).

Only a handful were converted. Seemingly no church was started at that time. Yet Dionysius, a distinguished member of the judicial court, became a believer. Tradition says he was the first bishop of Athens. A woman named Damaris and "some other people" also became converts (Acts 17:34, GNT). The Holy Spirit was at work.

How do you think Paul felt following his scholarly speech at the Areopagus when only a handful were converted?

A Savior Who Condescends

We have looked at Paul's first European churches, especially Philippi, through Luke's eyes. Now we look at the Philippian church through Paul's correspondence. Time had elapsed. Perhaps the church began about A.D. 51. The letter was written from prison in Caesarea or Ephesus, or perhaps from Rome eight to twelve years later.

Paul loved the Philippian church. He visited it again on his third missionary journey and sent a continual stream of coworkers to give encouragement. The letter is full of good will, prayer, and joyful memories. Watch for signs of maturing in Paul and the church. The letter came from Paul and Timothy; it is addressed "to all . . . who are God's people in Christ Jesus, along with your supervisors and servants" (Philippians 1:1).

Why did he write this letter? Paul wanted to tell them how much he loved them, how he longed to be with them, and how he hoped they would continue to grow in love (1:3-11). He was like a father urging a child to keep growing. He allayed their fears about his imprisonment, for he argued that he was happy to be making a strong witness. Paul spoke of being torn in two directions, whether to leave this world and live with Christ or stay, continue the work, and enjoy watching them grow (1:23-24).

When Paul alluded to "enemies" (1:28), he began to think of disharmony. Oh, how he hated disunity, dissension, and arrogant behavior. His appeal to them to live in harmony, not to think of their own affairs, but to see things from other people's point of view led him to a hymn. Most scholars believe that Philippians 2:5-11 was an early hymn, or song of faith, used in the churches to celebrate the humility of Jesus. Read it aloud to feel the beauty and sense of worship. Jesus became a slave, dying like a common criminal for our sakes. What a condescending,

NOTES

vulnerable Savior. What an offense to the proud. What a salvation for the humble.

How do these words about the Savior strike you as you read them out loud?

A Shout of Joy

Paul learned that some people were undermining the pure gospel he taught. Who were they? "Those who insist on circumcision, which is really mutilation" (Philippians 3:2), were those conservative Jewish Christians who still insisted on circumcision. Paul refused to budge because Christians are either saved by grace and grace alone or else they fall back into a religion of works-righteousness. For the circumcisers, it perhaps meant only a righteous act; but for Paul it meant accepting all of the requirements of the law of Moses (see Galatians 5:1-12).

Some of these leaders must have been bragging about their credentials, so Paul boasted of his Jewish roots (Philippians 3:4-6). If they wanted the full Law, Paul kept it better than they. Paul learned that legalism leads to despair, so he considered all that he had lost as "sewer trash" when compared to Christ (3:8; see Romans 1:16-17).

What moralisms or practices of works-righteousness do some people try to lay on new converts today?

Paul also criticized another group who were "enemies of the cross" (Philippians 3:18). They are more difficult to identify but seem to have been libertines, those who, by gluttony or drunkenness or self-indulgence, lacked discipline. "Their god is their stomach . . . their thoughts focus on earthly things" (3:19).

He wrote about these saved-by-grace free spirits also in Galatians 5:16-21. What would be libertine practices within the church today that violate the spirit of the gospel?

We don't know who Euodia and Syntyche were, but Paul wanted his church to live in perfect harmony and asked these two to settle their differences (Philippians 4:2).

Paul concluded his letter with a shout of joy. Even though he was in prison, even though he had learned to live in plenty or in poverty, the church had been gracious to remember him. Twice they sent help. Now they have helped him again. Then he reminded them, "God will meet your every need out of his riches in the glory that is found in Christ Jesus" (4:19). "Be glad in the Lord always! Again I say, be glad!" (4:4).

INTO THE WORLD

As you think about your life, it is easy to feel joy when things are going well. But what about when things are tough, situations are uncertain, and happiness seems like a distant memory? How do you have joy in spite of your circumstances? Paul encourages the church at Philippi to have joy in spite of their circumstances. As followers of Christ, we are to be agents of joy. How can you bring joy to others who are going through a difficult situation?

How can you take Paul's concept of joy into your world?

God's Word in My World

In what new ways will this session's message from God's Word influence my daily thoughts, attitudes, and actions so I continue to become more like Christ?

I will commit to integrating the above response into my daily living beginning this week by following this specific, measurable action:

IF YOU WANT TO KNOW MORE

We skipped quickly over Thessalonica. Read Paul's letters of encouragement to the Thessalonians, especially 1 Thessalonians 4:1-12 and 2 Thessalonians 3. The Thessalonian letters are the earliest letters written by Paul and the earliest writings in the New Testament.

"One night the Lord said to Paul in a vision, 'Don't be afraid. Continue speaking. Don't be silent. I'm with you and no one who attacks you will harm you, for I have many people in this city.'"

—Acts 18:9-10

10 Staying Strong Through Trials

OUR HUMAN CONDITION

If we look at the practice of Christianity from the outside, it's easy to walk away. Even within the church some people offer conflicting ideas about how to live as Christians. And then, God begins threatening our lifestyles—our use of words, money, time, relationships, things. . . . How do we stay strong when our Christian beliefs and lifestyles are threatened?

My commitment for "God's Word in My World" from our last session is:

ASSIGNMENT

As you read Acts, remember that you are reading the story the way Luke wants to tell it. In Second Corinthians the issues in the church seem more subtle. The advice Paul gives is profoundly personal, superbly spiritual. In Ephesians, we learn how we are to live for Christ and how to equip ourselves for the spiritual battles in our lives.

SPIRITUAL DISCIPLINES

Service

To live as servant in relationship is to desire the good of others, to value people above things, and to count no opportunity to serve as unworthy.

How can I serve even when I go through trials?

How will I practice this discipline this week?

Sabbath

Think for a few moments about gods in our society that almost everyone worships. What are their claims? How do they try to control our lives? When we cease work and rest for one day, we gain strength to stay strong through trials.

Prayer

Pray daily before study:

"Oh, I must find rest in God only,
    because my hope comes from him!
Only God is my rock and my salvation—
    my stronghold!—I will not be shaken.
My deliverance and glory depend on God.
    God is my strong rock.
    My refuge is in God" (Psalm 62:5-7).

Prayer concerns for the week:

Day 1 **Read Acts 18** (Paul in Corinth);
2 Corinthians 1–4 (Paul's crisis with Corinth, ministers of a new covenant, Resurrection life).

Day 2 **Read 2 Corinthians 5–8** (ministry of reconciliation, joy over repentance, collections).

Day 3 **Read 2 Corinthians 9–13** (generosity encouraged, false apostles, thorn in the flesh).

Day 4 **Read Acts 19** (Paul's ministry in Ephesus); **Acts 20:1–21:14** (goodbye to Ephesian leaders, on to Jerusalem); **Ephesians 1–2** (fullness of time).

Day 5 **Read Ephesians 3–4** (mystery of Christ, new life); **Ephesians 5–6** (subject to one another, whole armor of God).

Day 6 **Read "Into the Word" and "Into the World" and answer the questions or provide responses.**

Day 7 **Rest, pray, and attend class.**

INTO THE WORD

In Paul's day, power lived in Rome, culture flourished in Athens, but Corinth was where the action was. Every religion, every superstition, every debauchery known to humankind thrived in this frontier seaport. The city bubbled with energy, with new money, with peacetime prosperity.

Paul in Corinth

By the time of Paul's visit in A.D. 50 or 51, the population of Corinth had expanded to two hundred thousand freemen and three to four hundred thousand slaves. In A.D. 49 the emperor Claudius expelled all Jews from Rome because of Christian-Jewish disputes and riots within the synagogues. Many Jews fled to Corinth and formed at least one large synagogue there.

Paul could have caught a sailboat, or he may have walked overland the fifty miles from Athens to Corinth. As usual, he immediately located the Jewish quarter. There he met Aquila and Priscilla, Jewish Christians expelled from Rome who had arrived recently in Corinth. They, like Paul, were tentmakers. They took Paul right into their house.

Aquila and Priscilla were gracious, hospitable, and generous. Wherever they moved—Corinth, Ephesus, and back to Rome again—their house became a church and the gospel flourished. Paul called her by a Latin name, perhaps nickname, "Prisca" (2 Timothy 4:19). Usually Luke and Paul placed her name first. Was she of high social status, or did she increasingly take a leadership role, or both?

Of course, each Sabbath Paul and his friends attended synagogue, teaching and disputing with Jews and God-fearing Greeks (Acts 18:4). Then Silas and Timothy caught up, coming directly from Macedonia. The rift in the synagogue became so severe and the resistance to Paul's teachings so strong that Paul walked out. He went next door to a Greek named Titus or Titus Justus, shouting, "From now on I'll go to the Gentiles!" (18:6). God, in a vision, assured Paul not to be afraid, to push on with his message, "for I have many people in this city" (18:10). So Paul worked there, courageously and with lots of help, for a year and a half (18:11).

Notice a shift, not only from Jew to Gentile, but from synagogue to home. Household fellowship pervaded Jerusalem Christianity; household hospitality expressed itself in Asia Minor and Macedonia. But now house churches began to develop. After all, the Christians had no church buildings, and the synagogues were slowly closing to them. Soon in Paul's letters he would refer to "the church that meets in their house" (1 Corinthians 16:19). The positive effect was that intimacy, prayer, healing, and love flourished in the small groups. On the negative side, the variety of household groups, producing different leaders and holding diverse viewpoints, were sometimes divisive.

A Straightforward Gospel

Paul began by giving comfort. Corinthians were suffering soul pain. Those who suffer can receive comfort from God, from Christ who suffered for us. The glory is that, once comforted, people are able to comfort others as God comforts us.

The Corinthians were being confused by some preachers who claimed special knowledge. Like some Gnostics, they boasted of hidden truths. Like some members of mystery cults, they hinted at secret experiences. Paul asserted that his gospel was always straightforward. "We have conducted ourselves with godly sincerity and pure motives in the world" (2 Corinthians 1:12). Paul, and his gospel, have nothing to hide.

Paul's preaching and his letters have no double meanings. Paul was pointing to ways Christians ought to behave. Even his decision to delay another visit was not fickle. He would come. Then he proclaimed that Jesus is not yes and no. He is the divine Yes, for "all of God's promises have their yes in him" (1:20).

So much religion today seems phony. Some forms of Christianity prostitute the gospel. What is authentic Christian life and practice?

In what situations today might we need courage to be straightforward and truthful in the gospel we share?

The Invisible Is Eternal

How does one eliminate boasting about money, education, or success? Paul chose two ways. First, he showed how he and other apostles and missionaries were winning eternal glory by their sufferings. Our bodies, that is, our lives, are like "clay pots" (2 Corinthians 4:7). No boasting there. But the treasure, the priceless treasure, the saving Spirit of Jesus—now that is something to boast about. The power belongs to God and not to us. That gives us courage to live, courage to die. We may be "knocked down, but we aren't knocked out" (4:9). The reason we never collapse is because the inner person is receiving fresh strength.

The second way Paul undercut those who boasted of human achievements and appearances was with his stress on the ultimate and the eternal. The world looks at the size of your house, visible and transitory. But everyone knows that what is important is the quality of love in your home, invisible and permanent. The world admires fine speeches, but everyone knows the essential ingredient is whether the message is true. The world admires a handsome physical body, but everyone knows that what really matters is what is in the heart. "The things that can be seen don't last, but the things that can't be seen are eternal" (4:18).

This courage is not Stoic courage but is a hope in Christ, a hope that gives us an endurance the world cannot understand. "We are always confident" (5:6). But more, we want to spread that hope to others, not commending ourselves but commending our Savior. God "gave us the ministry of reconciliation" (5:18). Whenever we help another person discover this hope, worldly boasting disappears; and that person finds himself or herself at peace with God. The acceptable time for that to happen is right now.

Because this ministry of reconciliation is the responsibility of every Christian, we should not link up with unbelievers. This verse (6:14) is usually interpreted to mean marriage. But it means all sorts of yoking—business, social, family. In other places the Bible encourages us to remain in the world, associating with all sorts of people. But to be yoked with an unbeliever may destroy our own faith or may hinder our ministry.

What kind of courage is called for to be "in this world" and yet "not of this world," not yoked to unbelievers?

How would you describe the courage and faith Paul had that allowed him to keep on preaching and believing even when he passed through trials and his "thorn" was not taken away?

How can you have that kind of courage?

The temple of Artemis, one of the seven wonders of the ancient world, ruled the social and religious life of Ephesus. Artemis, called Diana by the Romans, stood proudly as mother goddess of fertility and protector of the city. Her statue, or part of it, was believed to have been a meteorite that dropped from heaven more than a thousand years earlier (Acts 19:35). Her magnificent temple was the pride of the city and the talk of the world. A religion linked with a culture for over a thousand years would be hard to displace.

The Holy Spirit

Religious beliefs and practices from all over the world surfaced in this great metropolis of well over half a million people. But worship of Artemis was the civil religion to which almost every citizen gave honor. The Jewish quarter, with permanent synagogues, was home for over fifty thousand Jews. They avoided conflict as much as possible, quietly maintaining their own traditions and practices.

Paul and his tentmaker friends, Priscilla and Aquila, stepped off the sailboat from Corinth and Paul immediately made contact with the synagogue (Acts 18:19). (Paul did not mean exactly what he said when he washed his hands of the Jews in Corinth.) In Ephesus Paul either softened his approach, or else the attitudes in the synagogue were more congenial. He "interacted with the

Jews" (18:19). "They asked him to stay longer" with them; so he promised, "God willing, I will return" (18:20-21).

Apollos came from Alexandria, home of thousands of Jews for centuries (18:24). Greek Judaism centered there; the Septuagint was translated there.

Apollos, a Jewish convert to Jesus, still had much to learn. Even though he was highly educated in Egyptian scholarship and the Hebrew Scriptures, his knowledge of Jesus was limited. His water baptism, perhaps the baptism of John, was for repentance. Priscilla and Aquila drew him aside and shared with him further information about Jesus, including the promise and power of the Holy Spirit (18:26). This lay couple brought into the Christian mission one of the ablest scholars and preachers of the early church.

Apollos traveled on to Corinth, doing such strong work, particularly reinterpreting the Hebrew Scriptures, that some Corinthian Christians preferred his preaching to Paul's. They chose sides, creating division.

Paul, in his letter to Corinth from Ephesus, pleaded for unity. "I planted," he said, "Apollos watered, but God made it grow" (1 Corinthians 3:6).

When Paul returned to Ephesus, beginning his third missionary journey, the immediate problem was one that confronts so many of our churches today. "Did you receive the Holy Spirit when you came to believe?" (Acts 19:2). The Ephesian Christians, like Apollos earlier, answered "We've not even heard that there is a Holy Spirit" (19:2).

When Paul placed his hands on the heads of the twelve men after they had been baptized in the name of Jesus, "The Holy Spirit came on them" (19:6). The moment reenacted Pentecost (2:4) in a small way and reminds us of the time that Peter preached to Cornelius (10:44).

For three months, Paul "offered convincing arguments" in the synagogue (19:8), but gradually doctrinal differences with the Jews widened. Paul and the believers moved into a lecture hall where interested Jews and Gentiles could meet daily (19:9).

Christians remained a part of synagogue life in many cities for about thirty more years. But after the destruction of the Temple in A.D. 70, Judaism consolidated synagogue life. About A.D. 85, the lines became firmly drawn. The Christian Jews were gradually shut out.

The Riot at Ephesus

Paul labored in Ephesus over part of three years (Acts 20:31), his longest stay in one place. The city exploded with emotion when a distinguished businessman, Demetrius, claimed the Christians were undermining the miniature temple and trinket industry (Acts 19:23-27). The Jews, after centuries of painful experience, had learned to walk by the idols in silence; but the enthusiastic new Christians boasted that the gods were no gods at all. Silversmiths belonged to craft guilds. Demetrius crafted silver replicas of the temple, silver statues of Artemis, charms, necklaces, amulets, and trinkets. He bought metal from the silver merchants, hired artisans and craft workers, sold to wholesalers all over the world. He had local retail outlets and on-the-street hucksters. Christians had often been in trouble over theology, sometimes over politics; now they were in trouble over economics. Nothing upsets people quite so much as an attack on their wallet.

Demetrius, the labor union, the chamber of commerce, and the local priests spread the word. Thousands gathered at the amphitheater, screaming like a sports crowd. Picture the huge mob shouting for two solid hours, "Great is Artemis of the Ephesians!" (19:34). People who forgot to burn incense before her altar or scarcely would give a dime for her expenses yelled because it was the patriotic thing to do. Their goddess was threatened; the security of their city was in danger. Religion, business, and patriotism were yoked in the silver statues; and all were under attack.

Luke used this story to show Paul's troubles with mounting resistance. In this case the town clergy reminded the mob that the law courts were open if anyone had defamed the temple of Artemis and that the unruly crowd was liable to a Roman crackdown for disturbing the peace.

Opposition to public procedures or political policies may seem anti-God or anti-country. Where do you see contemporary Christians, around the world or at home, in conflict with temples, politics, and business?

Children of Light

In many passages of Scripture, light is contrasted with darkness. Paul wanted the Ephesians to know that Christianity is not a set of do's and don'ts but that in Christ a whole new way of living was open to them—life in the light (Ephesians 5:8-9). Do you recall Jesus' parable of the evil spirit who brought back other evil spirits because the house had no good and proper resident (Luke 11:24-26)? Paul wrote, "Be filled with the Spirit," pray, sing songs, give thanks (Ephesians 5:18-20). Then fornication, greed, vulgar talk, and idolatry will not be a part of your lives (5:3-5).

Movies, television, music, and magazines are saturated with vulgarity. Sex and violence permeate the media. How can we avoid this lack of light?

Paul gives us instructions on how to live. How can we bring the light of Christ into the darkness that surrounds us?

INTO THE WORLD

Unity may be an act of courage; certainly it is an act of humility. Where have you seen unity as an act of courage?

At the deepest level, Christian stewardship is total and personal. One disciple's ministry was different from another's. How can we give the talents that we have?

Across the centuries, Christians have often lived in tension with their society's economic, political, or social practices. Where do you see tensions developing today?

If you take a stand for Christ what would you need to have courage?

God's Word in My World

In what new ways will this session's message from God's Word influence my daily thoughts, attitudes, and actions so I continue to become more like Christ?

I will commit to integrating the above response into my daily living beginning this week by following this specific, measurable action

IF YOU WANT TO KNOW MORE

Philemon was a slaveowner; Onesimus was a runaway slave. Both became Christians. Read their story in Paul's letter to Philemon. Paul advised the slave to return and the owner to be kind. What are your thoughts about how we are to understand this letter?

NOTES

"I wasn't disobedient to that heavenly vision. Instead, I proclaimed first to those in Damascus and Jerusalem, then to the whole region of Judea and to the Gentiles. My message was that they should change their hearts and lives and turn to God, and that they should demonstrate this change in their behavior."
—Acts 26:19-20

11 Boldness for the Gospel

OUR HUMAN CONDITION

Most of us try to slow down brave souls who risk the unknown. We say, "Be careful." "Don't go; it's dangerous." "You'll get into trouble if you do that." Perhaps we're fearful ourselves, maybe even ashamed that we are not willing to lay our own lives on the line.

My commitment for "God's Word in My World" from our last session is:

ASSIGNMENT

By now you know certain Jewish and Roman customs. Notice how carefully Paul tried not to offend the Jews. Observe how he used his "trials" not to gain freedom but to give testimony.

Luke began Acts by quoting Jesus: "You will be my witnesses in Jerusalem, in all Judea and Samaria, and to the end of the earth." Luke closes Acts with Paul preaching in Rome.

SPIRITUAL DISCIPLINES

Guidance
We make way for the guidance of the Holy Spirit when we are open, seeking, and receptive.

What shall I do to seek the guidance of the Holy Spirit?

How will I practice this discipline this week?

Sabbath
Sabbath is clearly at odds with what the world terms success. I am not in prison, but some are. I am not on trial, but some are. I am not being beaten, but some are. I am not being martyred, but some are. Today I will pray for Christians who are persecuted for righteousness' sake, all over the world.

Prayer
Pray daily before study:

"I will bless the LORD who advises me;
    even at night I am instructed
    in the depths of my mind.
I always put the LORD in front of me;
    I will not stumble because he is on
        my right side" (Psalm 16:7-8).

Prayer concerns for the week:

Day 1 **Read Acts 20:1–21:16** (toward Jerusalem).

Day 2 **Read Acts 21:17-40; 22** (arrest and defense).

Day 3 **Read Acts 23–24** (Jewish and Roman trials).

Day 4 **Read Acts 25–26** (appeal to Caesar, before King Agrippa).

Day 5 **Read Acts 27–28** (Paul sails for Rome); **Romans 1:1-17; 14–16** (earlier words of greeting from his Roman letter).

Day 6 **Read "Into the Word" and "Into the World" and answer the questions or provide responses.**

Day 7 **Rest, pray, and attend class.**

DISCIPLE FAST TRACK

INTO THE WORD

The air bristles with urgency. Luke's drama moves toward its climax. Paul, like Jesus, set his face toward Jerusalem. Everyone warned him not to go. They begged. They wept. Paul finally insisted that they stop, for their appeals were breaking his heart (Acts 21:13). The prophet Agabus, the same man who had foretold the famine, now prophesied Paul's imprisonment. Watch him carefully. He removed Paul's waist sash, or belt, symbolically bound up his own hands and feet, showing what would happen to Paul in the Holy City (21:10-11). Paul even admitted that the Holy Spirit had given warnings of the trouble he would face if he proceeded (20:23). Yet he had to complete the task of testifying to the gospel of God's grace (20:24).

Do you recall Philip the evangelist, who with Stephen was chosen to "serve tables"? Do you remember his powerful preaching in Samaria when he converted Simon the Great? Have you fixed in your memory his history-making influence on the Ethiopian eunuch?

Now we meet Philip again as Paul's host (21:7-9). For twenty-five years Philip worked and witnessed in Caesarea, that Roman garrison seaport town where Cornelius received the Holy Spirit. His home was a hostel for Christians coming and going to Asia and Europe. For Paul, Philip's home in Caesarea was a link with the Jerusalem church.

Paul planned to be in Philippi for Passover and in Jerusalem for Pentecost. In those intervening fifty days Paul expected to visit a dozen churches, travel by boat along the eastern coastline of the Mediterranean, and be on the steps of the Temple for the anniversary of the Holy Spirit explosion.

Passover was the first day of the Feast of Unleavened Bread. Observe that no mention is made of Good Friday or Easter. (The Crucifixion and Resurrection had taken place during Passover.) As yet they were not set aside as holy days. Every sermon included the Crucifixion; every Lord's Day celebrated Easter. The all-night meeting in Troas when they gathered "for a meal" (20:7) underlined Paul's intensity and urgency. So did his farewell fellowship on the beach with the Ephesian elders. He avoided the delay of going into the city itself (20:36-38). Paul would not be sidetracked or detained.

From a human point of view, several arguments must have played in Paul's mind for why he should not to go to Jerusalem. His work certainly was not completed: Corinth continued to be confused and divided. Ephesus needed mature leadership. Philippi and other Macedonian churches needed sound teaching. But an ever greater mission spurred Paul on. He was an initiator, a "church starter," a groundbreaker. He was called to plant; others would water. Paul wanted to take the gospel to Spain, to the very edges of the civilized world. Read Romans 15:23-29 to understand that he wanted to go to Rome as a base of operations for going to Spain. The Christian community in Rome had thrived

NOTES

for a decade. Paul encouraged them but wanted to break new ground. Burning in his soul were the words of Jesus, "You will be my witnesses . . . to the end of the earth" (Acts 1:8).

Yet Paul had to go to Jerusalem. Luke said that, even though the Spirit warned of trouble, the Spirit constrained him to go. What was driving Paul? Why was he so utterly convinced this journey was God's will for him?

We must not forget what Paul had been doing. He had gathered up an offering for the suffering saints in Jerusalem. From Philippi and Thessalonica, from Corinth and Ephesus, from church after church over a period of several years, he had been soliciting, pleading, encouraging, even cajoling, to raise the money. Why? Because he had promised. In fact, as he wrote to the Galatians, the offering had become for him the seal of the Jerusalem Council (Galatians 2:9-10). Receding in his mind were the requirements stated by James; those were easy and had become accepted practice. Now the promise of the offering for the poor must be fulfilled.

Why not send a messenger instead of going personally? He certainly had trusted others with money before. The answer is written between the lines in the account of Paul's arrival in Jerusalem (Acts 21:17-26). Would the offering from the Gentiles be accepted? Could the Jewish Christians and the Gentile Christians be held together? At stake was the unity of the Christian church. All sorts of rumors and false tales were circulating. Paul, and Paul alone, must interpret to James and the others what was happening. The money had to be properly delivered and the missionary work interpreted.

When have you known there would be consequences for sharing your faith, but felt you must go ahead anyway?

A Stormy Arrival

What happened when Paul explained the great outpouring of Spirit among the Gentiles? The beleaguered Judean Jewish Christians were thrilled at the report but not at the presence of Paul in Jerusalem (Acts 21:20-22). Right off they wanted to dispel rumors that Paul was profaning Judaism, teaching Jews not to circumcise, and ridiculing Jewish customs.

How could Paul symbolically show that he neither blasphemed Temple religion nor ridiculed the piety of Jewish Christians? Sometimes devout Jews took holy vows for a while. Paul had done that himself (18:18). They began by not cutting their hair. They concluded the vows with special purification rites and sacrifices at the Temple. If Paul, who had ended a vow himself only a short time before, would go to the Temple with four serious Jewish Christians for the seven-day rites of purification, if he would pay the money for the shaving of their heads, everyone would know he was still a good Jew (21:23-24). Paul agreed.

But to no avail. Somebody claimed that he had seen Paul take a Gentile, Trophimus, into the Temple (21:28-29). This was not true, but the whole city was aroused. A mob dragged Paul out of the Temple, into the streets. Only the quick action of the Roman soldiers saved his life (21:30-36).

Herod the Great had rebuilt an ancient fortress at the extension of the Temple area to do two things: to guard the city wall to the northeast and to oversee the Temple area from the high tower. Every day priests went to the fortress to check out their vestments for the day's activities. Commander Claudius Lysias, directly under the command of the procurator in Caesarea, was in charge.

On the steps of the barracks, Paul spoke courteously in educated Greek to Claudius. Notice the Roman officer's surprise that Paul was not an Egyptian Jew insurrectionist (21:37-39) and that Paul was a natural-born Roman citizen.

Paul then did an extraordinary thing. When he could have gone quietly into a cell, or possibly even have been freed, he asked to speak to the Jewish crowd (21:39). Amazing! What boldness. Why? Because he saw the opportunity to witness.

Paul switched to Aramaic, silenced the mob, reaffirmed his Jewish heritage, gave his Damascus road testimony, and reminded them of Stephen's martyrdom. They were quiet until he claimed God had told him to go to the Gentiles. Then they exploded in anger (22:21-22). They did not understand the promise to Abraham, the prophecy of Isaiah, and the mission of Jonah in the same way Paul did.

Later, when a perplexed Claudius "ordered" the Jewish Sanhedrin to hear Paul so that he could sort out the issues (22:30), Paul was bold to speak again. This time, he emphasized the Resurrection so strongly that Pharisees and Sadducees turned on each other (23:1-10).

That night, Paul heard the voice of God saying to him, "Be encouraged!" Paul had given testimony in Jerusalem; he would also witness in Rome (23:11).

In your life, when have you been bold for Christ, when have you felt like God was saying to you, "Be encouraged"?

In all our study of Paul, we have encountered no family. Suddenly a nephew appeared with secret information that saved Paul from ambush (23:16-22). Claudius properly and dutifully sent Paul to Felix the governor in Caesarea.

In Prison

Rome appointed Felix Antonius governor of Judea in A.D. 52. Normally the Romans appointed capable, experienced, and honest officials, but Felix was an exception. In the trial (Acts 24), the Jewish lawyer Tertullus tried flattery, but it sounded

NOTES

phony (24:2-8). Paul was more forthright, simply affirming Felix's experience as a judge and implying that the governor knew a good deal about Judaism. Paul limited his defense to his appropriate Jewish actions in Jerusalem: He came to worship. He disputed with no one. He brought alms for the poor. He offered sacrifices for purification. No Jew could be offended by those actions (24:10-21). Felix had no charge against him that would stand up under Roman law.

Felix would have freed Paul except for two reasons. Felix had offended the Jewish leaders so many times already. Once, in this time of great unrest, he had ruthlessly quelled a revolt by an Egyptian Jew, killing hundreds but letting the leader escape. That insurrectionist was the man Claudius Lysias thought Paul might be.

But also, Felix kept waiting for a bribe. He dangled Paul, but no money was forthcoming. So Felix left Paul in prison in Caesara for two years (24:27). Rome was so embarrassed by Felix's general administration that they recalled him in A.D. 60. Felix passed into oblivion.

Don't get the idea that Paul played games in his various defenses. He used every legitimate ploy. To the Jews he spoke Aramaic (Hebrew); to the Romans he spoke Greek. Before the Sanhedrin, made up of Sadducees who did not believe in resurrection and Pharisees who did, Paul deliberately divided them by focusing on their internal controversy. He claimed his Jewish background when suitable and his Roman citizenship when advantageous. His logic caused Festus to blurt out, "Too much learning is driving you mad!" (26:24).

The examination by flogging, which the tribune had prepared in Jerusalem, could have been life-threatening; so Paul claimed his Roman citizenship. When, after two years in prison, he appealed to the emperor, Paul hoped to get a fairer trial in Rome, especially when it appeared he might be tried again back in Jerusalem. Ready to die, Paul fought for every day of life. Notice that in each defense he also made a fervent witness for faith in Jesus Christ.

How have you been able to adjust your witness so that it appeals to different people in a variety of situations?

On Trial Again
Roman records call Festus an honorable governor. He arrived in Judea knowing the awful reputation of his predecessor Felix. He moved with dispatch, touching base with Jewish leaders in Jerusalem, looking at his prisoners, including Paul, held long on the docket, and trying to establish a favorable relationship with Herod Agrippa II.

Being new and without Jewish background, Festus was in deep water trying to follow the theological issues. He avoided the trap of

DISCIPLE FAST TRACK

transporting Paul to Jerusalem and set up a proper and immediate Roman proceeding (Acts 25:4-5). Paul, fearful that Festus would either turn him over to the Jews or change venue to Jerusalem, made a formal appeal to Caesar (25:9-11). Yet Festus did identify the conflict, more clearly than the Jewish leaders had, for it concerned a man named Jesus, raised from the dead (25:19).

Herod Agrippa II was only seventeen when his father died. Rome hesitated a few years and then gradually gave him territories traditionally under the Herods: Galilee, Samaria, areas around the Sea of Galilee, and east of the Jordan. With some Jewish blood, and much knowledge of the area, Herod Agrippa II tried to show support to Judaism by paving streets in Jerusalem with white marble. However, when the ultimate test came with Jewish rebellion in A.D. 66, Agrippa fully supported Rome.

The hearing before Festus, Herod Agrippa II, and Bernice was informal, for Paul had already appealed to Rome. Since Agrippa seemed curious, Paul seized the opportunity to testify to his religious experience, giving us our most complete account of his conversion (26:12-18).

In Paul's testimony, he shared the command from Jesus. "I am sending you [*to the Gentiles*] to open their eyes. Then they can turn from darkness to light and from the power of Satan to God, and receive forgiveness of sins and a place among those who are made holy by faith in me" (26:17-18). The missionary looked into the king's eyes and said, "I wasn't disobedient to that heavenly vision" (26:19). Then, with Governor Festus shaking his head, Paul zeroed in: "King Agrippa, do you believe the prophets? I know you do" (26:27). Everyone turned with amazement. For an instant, the king stood on trial before the Jewish evangelist in chains. "Are you trying to convince me that, in such a short time, you've made me a Christian?" asked the king (26:28). Paul responded that he wished everyone were a Christian, as he was, except for the chains (26:29). Luke again affirmed Paul's innocence with Agrippa's words that he "could have been released if he hadn't appealed to Caesar" (26:32). But God had whispered earlier to Paul that Paul would testify in Rome (23:11). Festus helped make it possible. (Remember that God used Pharaoh to feed the world through Joseph.)

Sailing for Rome

Sailing after mid-September was hazardous. After mid-November, treacherous. The winds turned tricky, the weather unpredictable, the late fall storms sudden and violent.

Luke speaks as "we" again in Acts 27:1, perhaps sharing the journey with Paul. Notice the details of every port en route as they stayed close to shore and then moved from island to island. The Roman centurion, Julius, treated Paul kindly on the journey. But neither he, the pilot, nor the shipowner listened to Paul's warnings (27:9-11).

Paul used even the storm as an opportunity to witness and prophesy. He said that God would not allow a loss of life and that

Paul would eventually stand before Caesar (27:22-25). Thus he gave faith messages even before a pagan audience.

Paul had written his letter to the church at Rome several years before, probably when he was in Corinth. Even though Romans is a theological treatise, provocative and forceful, aimed at a broader audience, Paul still had Rome in mind. If you read carefully the issues Paul addressed, especially as the letter opens and closes, you can detect between the lines the cosmopolitan mixture of issues already emerging.

The ship crashed on Malta, but all hands were safe (27:39-44). The island benefited from their arrival, for Paul survived a snakebite and healed the father of the island chief. The witness of the Holy Spirit continued to spread (28:1-10).

Finally Paul and his friends walked up the ancient Appian Way to Rome. His guard was light. Under house arrest for about two years, Paul witnessed to Jews and Romans alike.

When Paul summoned the Jewish leaders, he discovered that they did not know about the charges against him in Jerusalem (28:21). Furthermore, they listened to his arguments; though Paul was disappointed that only a few became believers (28:24-28). What happened in Asia Minor was now repeated in Rome.

We might think Luke's second volume would end with a report of Paul's death. But Luke's account has a different emphasis. Just as Jesus found many who would not believe, so did Paul. Paul quoted the prophet Isaiah: "You will hear, to be sure, but never understand. . . . / This people's senses have become calloused" (28:26-27).

Luke wanted his account to climax on that major theme. Paul continued for two years to proclaim "with complete confidence" God's kingdom and "to teach about the Lord Jesus Christ" (28:31), and the gospel continued its unstoppable progress.

INTO THE WORLD

Let's talk about jails. Most of us stay as far away from jails and prisons as we can, the teachings of Jesus notwithstanding. Is anyone from your church currently in jail? from your neighborhood?

Would it be possible to have a DISCIPLE FAST TRACK study in a nearby jail or prison? Ask a chaplain or warden. How might you help?

How do you proclaim the gospel in your world?

To help you share your faith story, write it out here.

God's Word in My World

In what new ways will this session's message from God's Word influence my daily thoughts, attitudes, and actions so I continue to become more like Christ?

I will commit to integrating the above response into my daily living beginning this week by following this specific, measurable action:

IF YOU WANT TO KNOW MORE

Paul, a Jew, knew that Israel was privileged to be God's covenant people. Yet, as a missionary, he knew that most of Israel rejected the gospel. Read carefully Romans 3–4 and 9–11 to discover Paul's belief that God will bring Israel into Christ.

"Instead, desire his kingdom and these things will be given to you as well."
—Luke 12:31

12 Ordering Our Lives

OUR HUMAN CONDITION

Mostly I put me first. Each new decision becomes a crisis; I feel pushed and pulled in all directions. I spend my time doing the immediate and put off the important. So often my life seems off balance.

My commitment for "God's Word in My World" from our last session is:

ASSIGNMENT

Remember Scriptures you have read that point to special priorities. Review biblical passages that focus on ways to arrange your life, to pattern it according to the ways of God. Think of priorities not listed here.

SPIRITUAL DISCIPLINES

Commitment

As we yield to God our life at its very center, whether in a moment or gradually, power becomes available for carrying out the commitment.

How do I turn my life over to God daily?

How will I practice this discipline this week?

Sabbath

Sabbath declares God is Lord and requires an ordering of priorities and a set of values different from those of the world around us.

Prayer

Pray daily before study:

"Lord, you have been our help,
    generation after generation.
Before the mountains were born,
    before you birthed the earth and
        the inhabited world—
    from forever in the past
    to forever in the future, you are
        God. . . .
Teach us to number our days
    so we can have a wise heart"
            (Psalm 90:1-2, 12).

Prayer concerns for the week:

Day 1 Read Exodus 20:1-6; Luke 12:22-34; Acts 4 and jot down your notes. Then turn in your Study Manual to "Day 1: God First" and answer the questions or provide responses.

Day 2 Read Psalm 92; Ecclesiastes 12:1-7; Exodus 20:8-11; Genesis 2:1-3; Deuteronomy 5:12-15; Exodus 25:1-8 and jot down your notes. Then turn in your Study Manual to "Day 2: Time" and answer the questions or provide responses.

Day 3 Read Exodus 35:4-5, 21-22; 36:5-7; 1 Corinthians 16:1-3; 2 Corinthians 9; Deuteronomy 26:1-15 and jot down your notes. Then turn in your Study Manual to "Day 3: Money" and answer the questions or provide responses.

Day 4 Read Ephesians 6:1-4; 5:21-33; Deuteronomy 6:1-9; 1 Corinthians 7 and jot down your notes. Then turn in your Study Manual to "Day 4: Family Responsibilities" and answer the questions or provide responses.

Day 5 Read Luke 8:40-48; 10:25-37; Acts 3:1-10 and jot down your notes. Then turn in your Study Manual to "Day 5: Openness to the Needs of Others" and answer the questions or provide responses.

Day 6 Answer the questions or provide responses under "God's Word in My World."

Day 7 Rest, pray, and attend class.

DISCIPLE FAST TRACK

INTO THE WORD, INTO THE WORLD

How do we synchronize our lives with the harmonies of the universe? How do we live in step with the rhythms of God? How can we time our thoughts and actions to mesh with *kairos*, God's time? How do we try to walk as disciples of Jesus the Christ?

Day 1: God First

In both Torah and Gospels we are admonished to put God first in our lives. Read again the first commandment in Exodus 20:1-3 or Deuteronomy 5:6-7. Explain what it means to you.

Read again Jesus' teaching to desire God's kingdom (Luke 12:22-31; Matthew 6:25-34). Put into words what you think Jesus meant when he said, "These things will be given to you as well" (Luke 12:31).

In Acts 4:13-22, when Peter and John were commanded to be silent, they responded, "It's up to you to determine whether it's right before God to obey you rather than God. As for us, we can't stop speaking about what we have seen and heard." Read this dramatic incident again. What does it say to you?

Day 2: Time

It is easy to believe something in general; the difficulty begins when we get specific. Consider time. How do we harmonize our timing with God's?

Just as the first fruits of harvest were dedicated to God, so the first breath of the new day can say, "Praise the Lord." The psalmist declared,

> "It is good to give thanks to the LORD . . .
>   to proclaim your loyal love in the morning"
>   (Psalm 92:1-2).

How are you organizing your life to speak first to God upon awakening?

John in the Revelation named Jesus "the Alpha and the Omega, the beginning and the end" (Revelation 21:6). Day's opening and closing whisper the name of Jesus. Paul urged the church in Ephesus not to let the sun go down on their anger. Don't go to sleep angry (Ephesians 4:26). Can you slip off anger, guilt, and fear as you undress yourself for the night? Describe your design for the closing time of day.

Genesis hints that Sabbath is written into the fabric of the universe, into the cells of our minds and bodies. Torah stresses Sabbath as a law of covenant. Read again the fourth commandment (Exodus 20:8-11). Jesus relaxed tight moralistic legislation, even saying that he was Lord of the Sabbath (Luke 6:5) and that the Sabbath was made for our benefit (Mark 2:27).

As you have discovered the many dimensions of Sabbath and have experimented with a variety of Sabbath expressions, what insights have you gained?

What are some habits you are developing?

As you studied the Tabernacle and became aware of Jesus' prayer life, what aspects of worship or prayer have become meaningful to you?

Day 3: Money

As with our time, both Old and New Testaments ask us to give first fruits to God. Read again Exodus 34:26a; 1 Corinthians 16:2; 2 Corinthians 9:6-9. One principle of the tithe is first fruits as well as proportionate giving. Jesus, in his warning to the Pharisees, did not abolish this mark of covenant. But he called them to task for focusing on the tithe while neglecting justice and love of God.

Yet Jesus reserved his praise for extravagant giving: Zacchaeus (Luke 19:8), the widow with two coins (21:1-4), and the woman who brought the alabaster jar of expensive ointment (7:36-50). Paul told the Corinthian church, "Everyone should give whatever they have decided in their heart. They shouldn't give with hesitation or because of pressure. God loves a cheerful giver" (2 Corinthians 9:7).

How well are you managing to put God first in your financial priorities?

Describe how open you are to generosity and hospitality in your giving.

If people are too poor, they are anxious over food, shelter, and clothing. If people are too rich, they are often anxious about their possessions. In what ways are you anxious over necessities or your possessions? How much time do you spend worrying about getting, keeping, and caring for necessities or possessions?

Day 4: Family Responsibilities

Families have different configurations, and new shapes at different times. Read again Exodus 20:12 and Ephesians 6:1-4. What does honor to parents mean to you at this moment?

Some disciples are married. What does Ephesians 5:22-33 mean to you?

In Genesis 2:21-24 and Ephesians 5:31, marriage seems to be a higher priority than obligation to parents. What do you think?

What parent ever feels totally successful? Read again Deuteronomy 6:1-9. How effective are you, as a parent or caregiver, in teaching the faith to children?

Some disciples are single. What did you think about Paul's teaching on singleness and marriage (1 Corinthians 7:8, 25-38)?

What family responsibilities do you have? How far can you extend your family concerns? (Recall Boaz and Ruth.)

Day 5: Openness to the Needs of Others

As you read Luke and Acts, you noticed so many ministries that were unplanned. So many acts of caring and compassion were a dividend of grace. Jesus was ready for the unexpected need.

Read Luke 8:40-48. On the way to the house of a leader of the synagogue, Jesus had time to heal a desperate woman.

In the parable of the good Samaritan (10:25-37), the Samaritan, caught off guard, was ready.

Peter and John were walking to the Temple to pray when they encountered the man who was lame (Acts 3:1-10).

Explain how the Christian disciple develops and maintains a posture of openness to others.

How can we work and play so that we are open to a quick change in what's important at the moment? How able are you to quickly shift gears in the face of human need?

The old teacher in Ecclesiastes recognized that different situations demand different responses. For enjoyment, read Ecclesiastes 3:1-14.

God's Word in My World

In what new ways will this session's message from God's Word influence my daily thoughts, attitudes, and actions so I continue to become more like Christ?

These are my priorities:

I will commit to integrating the above response into my daily living beginning this week by following this specific, measurable action:

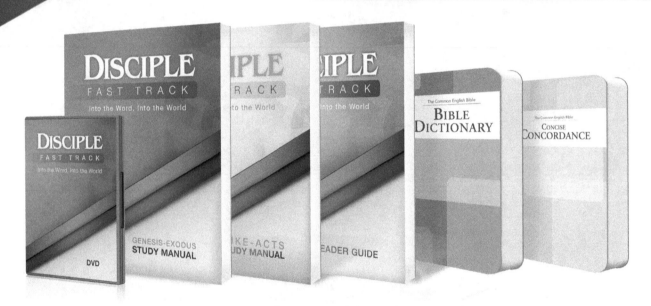

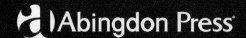

Here are all the studies in the
Disciple Bible Study Family!

Fast Track

Disciple

What study will you do next?
Learn more at adultbiblestudies.com/Disciple

Short-Term Disciple

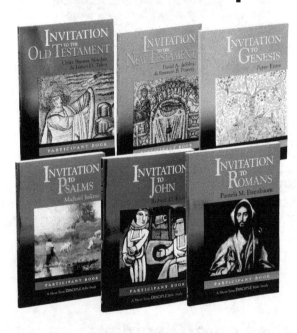

Other Studies

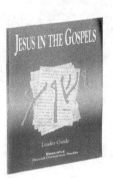

Jesus in the Gospels   Christian Believer

CPSIA information can be obtained
at www.ICGtesting.com
Printed in the USA
LVHW060316210822
726418LV00007B/207